W9-BZP-421

COATS Coats & Clark

GARMENTS
for beginners

Seams Sew Easy™

Copyright © 1998 Creative Publishing international, Inc.
5900 Green Oak Drive Minnetonka, Minnesota 55343 • 1-800-328-3895
All rights reserved • Printed in U.S.A.

CREATIVE
PUBLISHING
international

Contents

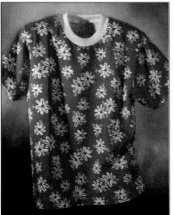

GARMENTS FOR BEGINNERS

Created by: The Editors of Creative Publishing international, Inc.

Library of Congress Cataloging-in-Publication Data
Garments for beginners.
    p. cm. -- (Seams sew easy)
  Includes index.
  ISBN 0-86573-328-7
  1. Tailoring (Women's) 2. Machine sewing. I. Creative
Publishing international. II. Series.
TT519.5.G37 1998
646.4'04--dc21   98-28741

Introduction

Welcome to the rewarding world of sewing. The *Seams Sew Easy*™ series of books is designed to encourage creativity and instill confidence as you learn to sew. Easy-to-follow instructions with colorful photographs and illustrations help you build your sewing skills while making garments and home decorating items that really appeal to you. This book will teach you how to sew them, and, in the process, you'll develop sewing skills that will help you tackle many other sewing projects with confidence.

The projects in this book are specifically designed for beginning sewers. However, it's exciting to know you can sew a well-rounded wardrobe for casual, dress, and business wear while sticking to relatively simple patterns.

Each project will teach you new skills, listed under WHAT YOU'LL LEARN. Throughout the book you will find tips and explanations to help you understand the "why" behind what you are doing. We have also shown variations for each project, encouraging you to explore the unlimited possibilities for design and fabric choices.

Use the first section of the book to acquaint yourself with your sewing machine and the techniques and supplies that encompass the art of sewing. Your sewing machine owner's manual is a necessity; refer to it first if you have questions or problems specific to your machine. The project directions in this book are meant to supplement and clarify your pattern directions. They may not follow your pattern directions exactly because there are often several techniques for performing the same sewing tasks. It is important to read through the pattern directions, in case your pattern has design details you should be aware of, such as side seam pockets or facings shaped differently than those we are showing. Pattern instruction sheets also have other valuable information specific to each pattern.

The first step in any sewing project is to read through the directions from beginning to end. Refer to the **Quick Reference** for definitions or elaborations on any words or phrases printed **like this** on the page. If the word or phrase is followed by a page number, its reference can be found on the page indicated. Words printed **LIKE THIS** can be found in the **GLOSSARY** on page 124. At the beginning of every project you will find a list telling you WHAT YOU'LL NEED. Read through the information on fabrics before you go shopping, so the fabric store will seem a little more user-friendly when you get there.

Above all, enjoy the process. Give yourself the opportunity to be creative, and express yourself through the clothes you sew.

The Sewing Machine

The principle parts common to all modern sewing machines are shown in the diagrams at right. The parts may look different on your model, and they may have slightly different locations, so open your owner's manual, also. If you do not have an owner's manual for your machine, you should be able to get one from a sewing machine dealer who sells your brand. Become familiar with the names of the parts and their functions. As you spend more time sewing, these items will become second nature to you.

If you are buying a new machine, consider how much and what kind of sewing you expect to do. Talk to friends who sew and to sales personnel. Ask for demonstrations, and sew on the machine yourself. Experiment with the various features while sewing on a variety of fabrics, including knits, wovens, lightweights, and denim. Think about the optional features of the machine and which ones you want on yours. Many dealers offer free sewing lessons with the purchase of a machine. Take advantage! These lessons will be geared to your particular brand and model of sewing machine.

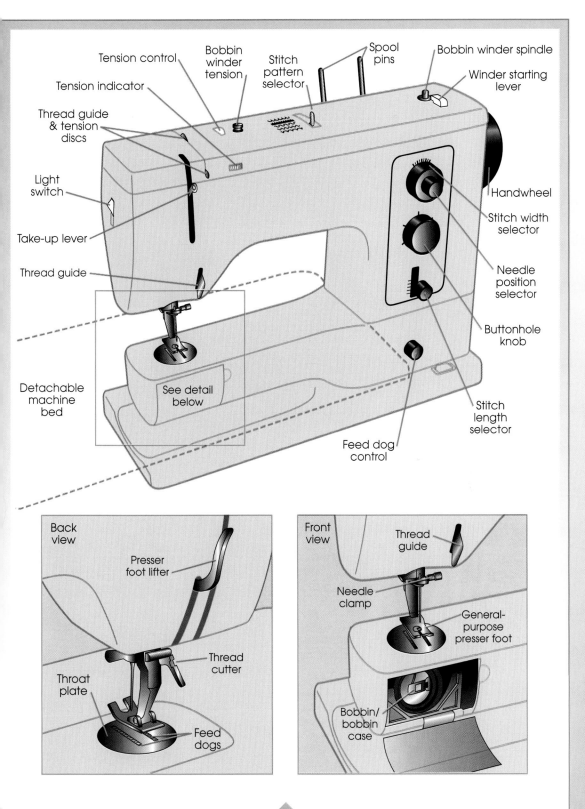

Tension control

Bobbin winder tension

Stitch pattern selector

Spool pins

Bobbin winder spindle

Tension indicator

Winder starting lever

Thread guide & tension discs

Light switch

Handwheel

Stitch width selector

Take-up lever

Needle position selector

Thread guide

Buttonhole knob

Detachable machine bed

See detail below

Stitch length selector

Feed dog control

Back view

Presser foot lifter

Thread cutter

Throat plate

Feed dogs

Front view

Thread guide

Needle clamp

General-purpose presser foot

Bobbin/ bobbin case

Machine *Accessories*

Sewing Machine Needles

Sewing machine needles come in a variety of styles and sizes. The correct needle choice depends mostly on the fabric you have selected. Sharp points **(A)**, used for woven fabrics, are designed to pierce the fabric. Ballpoints **(B)** are designed to slip between the loops of knit fabric rather than pierce and possibly damage the fabric. Universal points **(C)** are designed to work on both woven and knitted fabrics. The size of the needle is designated by a number, generally given in both European (60, 70, 80, 90, 100, 110) and American (9, 11, 12, 14, 16, 18) numbering systems. Use size 11/70 or 12/80 needles for any of the mediumweight fabrics you would find suitable for curtains. A larger number means the needle is thicker and that it is appropriate for use with heavier fabrics and heavier threads.

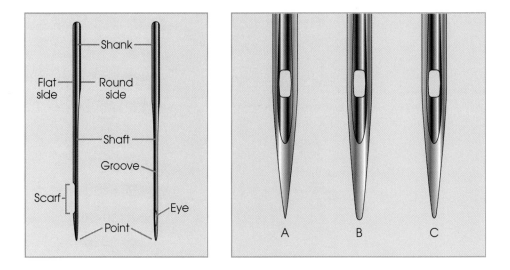

TIP: Though needle style and size are usually indicated in some way on the needle, it is often difficult to see without a magnifying glass, and you most likely will not remember what needle is in the machine. As an easy reminder, when you finish a sewing session, leave a fabric swatch from your current project under the presser foot.

Bobbins

Stitches are made by locking the upper thread with a lower thread, carried on a bobbin. Always use bobbins in the correct style and size for your machine. Bobbin thread tension is controlled by a spring on the bobbin case, which may be built in **(A)** or removable **(B).**

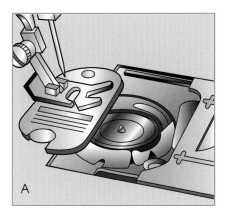

A

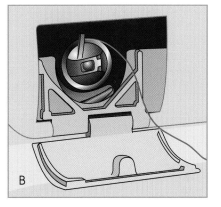

B

Presser Feet

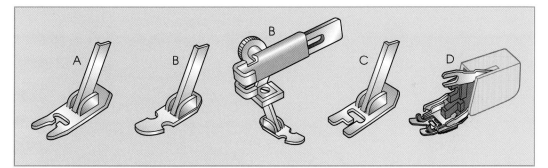

Every sewing machine comes with accessories for specialized tasks. More can be purchased as you develop your interest and skills. Your machine manual or dealer can show you what accessories are available and will explain how to use them to get the best results.

A general-purpose foot **(A),** probably the one you will use most often, has a wide opening to accommodate the side-to-side movement of the needle in all types of utility (nondecorative) stitches. It is also suitable for most straight stitching. A zipper foot **(B)** is used to insert zippers or to stitch any seam

that has more bulk on one side than the other. For some sewing machines, the zipper foot is stationary, requiring you to move the needle position to the right or left. For other styles, the position of the zipper foot itself is adjustable. A special-purpose or embroidery foot **(C)** has a grooved bottom that allows the foot to ride smoothly over decorative stitches or raised cords. Some styles are clear plastic, allowing you to see your work more clearly. A walking foot **(D)** feeds top and bottom layers at equal rates, allowing you to more easily match patterns or stitch bulky layers.

Getting *Ready to Sew*

Simple tasks of inserting the needle, winding the bobbin, and threading the machine have tremendous influence on the stitch quality and performance of your machine. Use this guide as a general reference, but refer to your owner's manual for instructions specific to your machine.

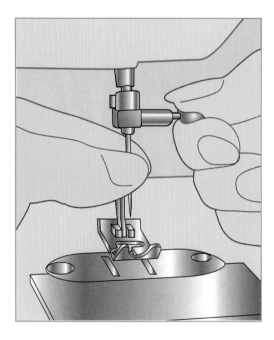 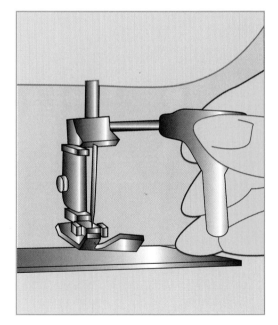

Inserting the Needle

Loosen the needle clamp. After selecting the appropriate needle for your project (page 8), insert it into the machine as high as it will go. The grooved side of the needle faces forward, if your bobbin gets inserted from the front or top; it faces to the left, if your bobbin gets inserted on the left. Tighten the clamp securely.

Winding the Bobbin

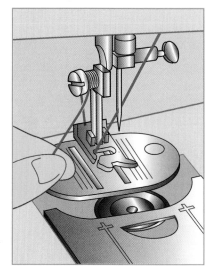

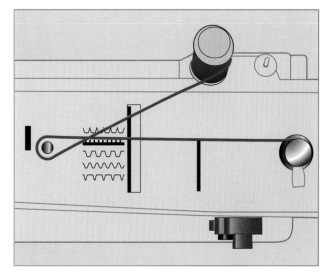

If the bobbin case is built in, the bobbin is wound in place with the machine fully threaded as if to sew (page 12).

Removable bobbins are wound on the top or side of the machine, with the machine threaded for bobbin winding, as described in your owner's manual.

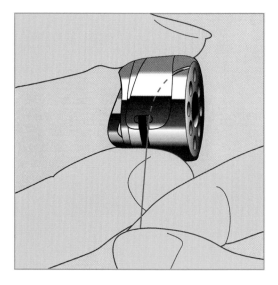

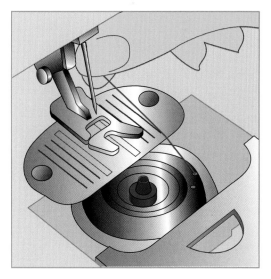

Bobbin thread must be drawn through the bobbin case tension spring. For wind-in-place bobbins, this happens automatically when you wind the bobbin, but you must do it manually when you insert a bobbin that already has thread on it.

continued

Threading the Machine

Because every sewing machine is different, the threading procedure for your machine may differ slightly from the one shown here. Once again, it is important to refer to your owner's manual. Every upper thread guide adds a little tension to the thread as it winds its way to the needle. Missing one of them can make a big difference in the quality of your stitches.

 Set the thread spool on the spindle.

A. Vertical spindle. Position the spool so that it will turn clockwise as you sew.

B. Horizontal spindle. The spool is held in place with an end cap. If your spool has a small cut in one end for minding the thread, position the spool with that end to the right.

TIP: If the spool is new and has paper labels covering the holes, poke them in, completely uncovering the holes, to allow the spool to turn freely.

Unless your machine has a self-winding bobbin, you will want to wind the bobbin before threading the machine (page 11).

 Pull the thread to the left and through the first thread guide.

 Draw the thread through the tension guide.

TIP: It is very important to have the presser foot lever up when threading the machine, because the tension discs are then open. If the presser foot is down and the discs are closed, the thread will not slide between the discs, and your stitches will not make you happy.

 Draw the thread through the next thread guide.

 Insert the thread through the take-up lever.

 Draw the thread through the remaining thread guides.

 Thread the needle. Most needles are threaded from front to back; some, from left to right.

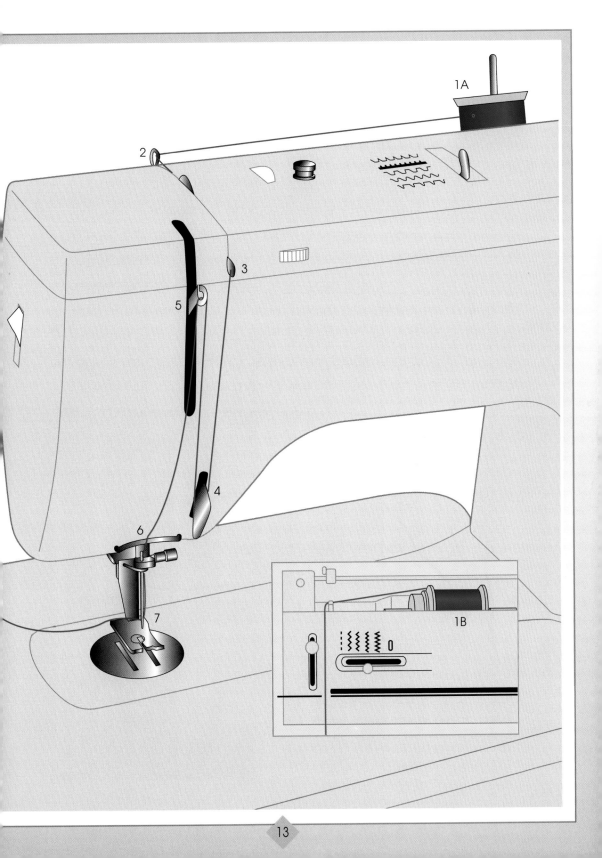

How to *Balance Tension*

Your machine forms stitches by interlocking the bobbin thread with the needle thread. Every time the needle goes down into the fabric, a sharp hook catches the needle thread and wraps the bobbin thread around it. Imagine this little tug-of-war. If the needle thread tension is "stronger" than the bobbin thread tension, the needle thread pulls the bobbin thread through to the top. If the bobbin thread tension is "stronger," it pulls the needle thread through to the bottom. When the tensions are evenly balanced, the stitch will lock exactly halfway between the top and bottom of the layers being sewn, which is right where you want it.

Some machines have "self-adjusting tension," meaning the machine automatically adjusts its tension with every fabric you sew. For machines that do not have this feature, you may have to adjust the needle thread tension slightly as you sew different fabrics.

Testing the Tension

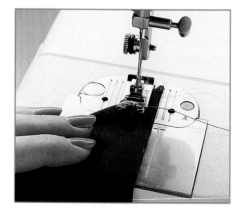

1 Thread your machine and insert the bobbin, using two very different colors of thread, neither of which matches the fabric. Cut an 8" (20.5 cm) square of a smooth, mediumweight fabric. Fold the fabric in half diagonally, and place it under the presser foot so the fold aligns to your 1/2" (1.3 cm) seam guide. Lower the presser foot and set your stitch length at 10 stitches per inch or 2.5 mm long.

2 Stitch a line across the fabric, stitching ½" (1.3 cm) from the diagonal fold. Remove the fabric from the machine. Inspect your stitching line from both sides. If your tension is evenly balanced, you will see only one color on each side. If you see both thread colors on the top side of your sample, the needle tension is tighter than the bobbin tension. If you see both thread colors on the back side of your sample, the bobbin tension is tighter than the needle tension.

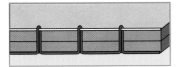

Top tension too tight

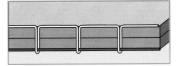

Top tension too loose

Tensions even

Adjusting the Tension

Before adjusting the tension on your machine, first check:
- that your machine is properly threaded (page 12)
- that your bobbin is properly installed
- that your needle is not damaged and is inserted correctly

3 Pull on your stitching line until you hear threads break. (Because you stitched on the **BIAS,** the fabric will stretch slightly.) If the thread breaks on only one side, your machine's tension is tighter on that side.

After checking these three things, you may need to adjust the tension on your machine. (Check your owner's manual.) Tighten or loosen the needle thread tension *slightly* to bring the needle thread and bobbin thread tensions into balance. Test the stitches after each adjustment, until you achieve balanced tension. If slight adjustments of the needle tension dial do not solve the problem, the bobbin tension may need adjusting. However, most manufacturers do not recommend that you adjust bobbin tension yourself, so unless you have received instructions for your machine, take your machine to the repairman.

Sewing a *Seam*

You may or may not be familiar with the very basic technique of running your machine and sewing a seam. Use this exercise as a refresher course whenever you feel you have lost touch with the basics or if your personal technique has become sloppy. Little frustrations, such as thread jams, erratic stitching lines, or having the thread pull out of the needle at the start of a seam, can often be prevented or corrected by following these basic guidelines. If you are really not sure where to begin, then you should probably begin right here!

1 Thread your machine (page 12) and insert the bobbin (page 11). Holding the needle thread with your left hand, turn the handwheel toward you until the needle has gone down and come back up to its highest point. A stitch will form, and you will feel a tug on the needle thread. Pull on the needle thread to bring the bobbin thread up through the hole in the throat plate. Pull both threads together under the presser foot and off to one side.

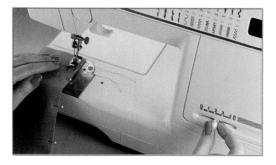

2 Cut rectangles of mediumweight fabric. Place the pieces right sides together, aligning the outer edges. Pin the pieces together along one long edge, inserting the pins about every 2" (5 cm), perpendicular to the edge. Place the fabric under the presser foot so the pinned side edges align to the 1/2" (1.3 cm) seam guide and the upper edges align to the back of the presser foot. Lower the presser foot, and set your stitch length at 2.5 mm, which equals 10 stitches per inch.

3 Begin by **backstitching** several stitches to the upper edge of the fabric. Hold the thread tails under a finger for the first few stitches. This prevents the needle thread from being pulled out of the needle and also prevents the thread tails from being drawn down into the bobbin case, where they could potentially cause the dreaded **thread jam.**

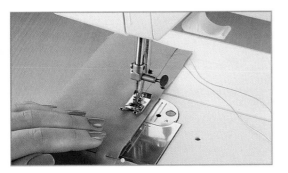

Backstitching secures the beginning and end of your stitching line so that the stitches will not pull out. The method for backstitching varies with each sewing machine. You may need to lift and hold your stitch length lever, push in and hold a button, or simply touch an icon. Check your owner's manual.

Stitch forward over the backstitched line, and continue sewing the 1/2" (1.3 cm) seam. Gently guide the fabric while you sew by walking your fingers ahead of and slightly to the sides of the presser foot. Remember, you are only guiding; let the machine pull the fabric.

Thread jams. No matter how conscientious you are at trying to prevent them, thread jams just seem to be lurking out there waiting to mess up your day. DON'T USE FORCE! Remove the presser foot, if you can. Snip all the threads you can get at from the top of the throat plate. Open the bobbin case door or throat plate, and snip any threads you can get at. Remove the bobbin, if you can. Gently remove the fabric. Thoroughly clean out the feed dog and bobbin area before reinserting the bobbin and starting over. Then just chalk it up to experience and get over it!

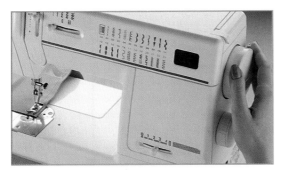

Stop stitching and remove pins as you come to them. When you reach the end of the fabric, stop stitching; backstitch several stitches, and stop again. Turn the handwheel toward you until the needle is in its highest position.

TIP: Straight stitching lines are easier to achieve if you watch the edge of the fabric along the seam guide and ignore the needle. Sew smoothly at a relaxing pace, with minimal starting and stopping, and without bursts of speed. You have better control of the speed if you operate your foot control with your heel resting on the floor.

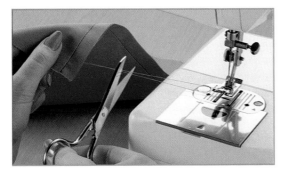

Raise the presser foot. Pull the fabric smoothly away from the presser foot, either to the left side or straight back. If you have to tug the threads, turn your handwheel slightly toward you until they pull easily. Cut the threads, leaving tails 2 1/2" to 3" (6.5 to 7.5 cm) long.

More About *Seams*

Aside from the standard straight-stitch **SEAM,** your machine is probably capable of sewing several other stitches that are appropriate for various fabrics and situations. Whenever you sew with knits, for example, you want a seam that will stretch with the fabric. To prevent raveling of woven fabrics, **SEAM ALLOWANCE** edges must be **FINISHED.** There are several finishing methods to choose from, depending on the fabric and the capabilities of your machine. These general guidelines will help you decide when to use these stitches and finishing methods. Your owner's manual is the best source of specific information for your machine.

Stretch Seams

> **TIP:** The cut edges of knit fabrics do not ravel, but they often curl. To minimize this problem, the seam allowances are usually finished together and pressed to one side.

Double-stitched seam. Stitch on the seamline, using a straight stitch set at a length of 12 stitches per inch, which equals 2 mm long. Stretch the fabric slightly as you sew, to allow the finished seam to stretch that much. Stitch again ⅛" (3 mm) into the seam allowance. Trim the seam allowance close to the second stitching line. This seam is appropriate for fabrics with minimal stretch or for seams sewn in the vertical direction on moderate stretch knits.

Narrow zigzag seam. Stitch on the seamline, using a very narrow zigzag stitch set at 12 stitches per inch, which equals 2 mm long. If the fabric is very stretchy in the direction you are sewing, you may also stretch the fabric slightly as you sew. Trim the seam allowance to ¼" (6 mm), if necessary. Set the zigzag wider, and stitch the seam allowance edges together. This seam is appropriate for very stretchy knits.

Built-in stretch stitch. Differing from brand to brand, these stitches are designed to incorporate stretch, so that you do not need to stretch the fabric as you sew. Some stitch styles, like the bottom two samples, are a pattern of zigzag and straight stitches that stitch and finish the seam in one pass. Check your manual for stitch settings.

Seam Finishes

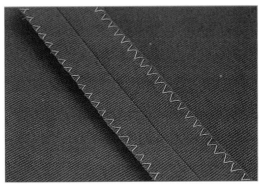

Stitched and pinked finish. Stitch ¼" (6 mm) from each seam allowance edge, using a straight stitch set at 12 stitches per inch, which equals 2 mm. Trim close to the stitching, using pinking shears (page 27). This finish is suitable for finely woven fabrics that do not ravel easily.

Zigzag finish. Set the zigzag stitch on or near maximum width and a length of 10 stitches per inch, which equals 2.5 mm. Stitch close to the edge of each seam allowance so that the right-hand stitches go just over the edge. If the fabric puckers, try a narrower zigzag width.

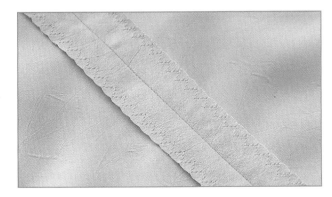

Multistitch-zigzag finish. If your machine has this stitch, check your owner's manual for directions on selecting the settings. Stitch near, but not over the edge of, each seam allowance.

Turn and zigzag finish. Set the zigzag stitch near maximum width at a length of 10 stitches per inch, which equals 2.5 mm. Turn under the seam allowance edge ⅛" to ¼" (3 to 6 mm). Stitch close to the folded edge so that the right-hand stitches go just on or over the fold. Use this finish on loosely woven fabrics, especially on garments, such as jackets, where the inside may be visible occasionally.

Hand Stitches

While modern sewers rely on sewing machines for speedy garment construction, there are situations when hand stitching is necessary or preferable. You may need to slipstitch an opening closed in the lining of a vest, or perhaps you like the look of a hand-stitched blind hem (page 22). Of course you'll also need to sew on buttons.

Threading the Needle

Insert the thread end through the needle's eye, for sewing with a single strand. Or fold the thread in half, and insert the fold through the eye, for sewing with a double strand. Pull through about 8" (20.5 cm). Wrap the other end(s)

around your index finger. Then, using your thumb, roll the thread off your finger, twisting it into a knot.

> **TIP:** Use a single strand when slipstitching or hemming. Use a double strand when sewing on buttons. To avoid tangles, begin with thread no longer than 18" (46 cm) from the needle to the knot. Run the thread through beeswax (page 25), if desired.

Slipstitching

 1 Insert the threaded needle between the seam allowance and the garment, just behind the opening. Bring it to the outside in the seamline. If you are right-handed, work from right to left; lefties work from left to right.

2 Insert the needle into the fold just behind where the thread came up, and run it inside the fold for about 1/4" (6 mm). Bring the needle out, and draw the thread snug. Take your next stitch in the opposite fold, inserting the needle directly across from the previous stitch.

3 Continue, crossing from one fold to the other, until you have sewn past the opening. Secure the thread with several tiny stitches in the seamline. Then take a long stitch, and pull it tight. Clip the thread at the surface, and let the tail disappear inside.

Sewing on a Shank Button

1 Place the button on the mark, with the shank hole parallel to the buttonhole. Secure the thread on the right side of the garment with a small stitch under the button.

2 Bring the needle through the shank hole. Insert the needle down through the fabric and pull the thread through. Take four to six stitches in this manner.

3 Secure the thread in the fabric under the button by making a knot or by taking several small stitches. Clip the thread ends.

Sewing on a Sew-through Button

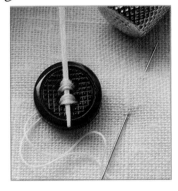

1 Place the button on the mark, with the holes lining up parallel to the buttonhole. Bring the needle through the fabric from the underside and up through one hole in the button. Insert the needle into another hole and through the fabric layers.

2 Slip a toothpick, match, or sewing machine needle between the thread and the button to form a shank. Take three or four stitches through each pair of holes. Bring the needle and thread to the right side under the button. Remove the toothpick.

3 Wind the thread two or three times around the button stitches to form the shank. Secure the thread on the right side under the button, by making a knot or taking several small stitches. Clip the threads close to the knot.

Hems

There are a number of ways to hem the lower edges of skirts, pants, jackets, and shirts. Some hems are sewn by machine; others by hand. The method you choose will depend on the fabric, the garment style, and your own preference. For methods that do not involve turning under the raw edge, **FINISH** the edge (page 19) in an appropriate manner, before hemming.

Hand Hems

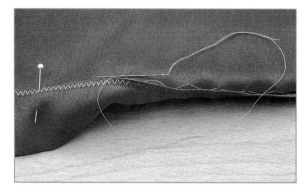

Blindstitch. Fold back the finished edge of the hem 1/4" (6 mm). Take a small stitch to anchor the thread in a seam allowance. Work with the needle pointing in the direction you are going. Take a very small horizontal stitch in the garment, catching only one or two threads. Take the next stitch in the hem, 1/4" to 1/2" (6 mm to 1.3 cm) away from the first stitch. Continue alternating stitches; do not pull too tightly.

Blind catchstitch. Fold back the finished edge of the hem 1/4" (6 mm). Take a small stitch to anchor the thread in a seam allowance. Work with the needle pointing in the direction opposite from the way you are going. Take a very small horizontal stitch in the garment, catching only one or two threads. Take the next stitch in the hem, 1/4" to 1/2" (6 mm to 1.3 cm) away from the first stitch, crossing the stitches. Continue alternating the stitches in a zigzag pattern.

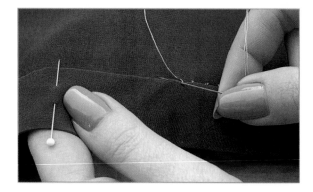

Slipstitch. Fold under the raw edge 1/4" (6 mm), and press. Take a small stitch to anchor the thread in a seam allowance. Work with the needle pointing in the direction you are going. Follow the directions for slipstitching on page 20, catching only one or two threads with each stitch that goes into the garment.

Machine Hems

A

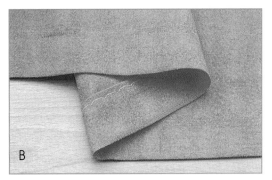

B

Machine blindstitch. Follow your manual for adjusting the stitch settings, and use the appropriate presser foot. Test the stitch on a scrap of the garment fabric until you are happy with the results. **A** Place the hem allowance facedown on the machine bed, with the bulk of the garment folded back. Allow about ¼" (6 mm) of the hem edge to extend under the presser foot, aligning the soft fold to rest against the guide in the foot. Stitch along the hem, close to the fold, catching only one or two threads of the garment with each left-hand stitch of the needle. **B** When complete, open out the hem, and press it flat.

Double-fold hem. This method results in one or two rows of straight stitches showing on the right side of the garment, which is generally a more casual appearance. Follow page 56, steps 14 and 15 or page 106, steps 2 and 3. This method is most successful on straight edges where there is no excess fullness to ease in. It may be helpful to hand-baste the folds in place before machine-stitching.

Double-needle hem. Stitched from the right side of the fabric, this hem is suitable for knit garments, because it will stretch slightly. The farther apart the needles are spaced, the more stretch the hem will have. However, widely spaced needles will usually produce a ridge between the stitching lines. Using two thread spools on top, thread both needles. Place tape on the bed of the machine as a stitching guide.

Sewing Supplies

Garment construction involves many steps: measuring, laying out the pattern, cutting, marking, stitching, and pressing. For each of these steps there are special tools and supplies to make your sewing easier and help you complete your projects successfully. Don't feel you need to buy all the items before you start. For instance, a pair of sharp shears and a seam ripper will see you through most of the cutting tasks for the projects in this book. You will undoubtedly acquire additional tools as your skills and interests grow.

Hand-sewing Supplies

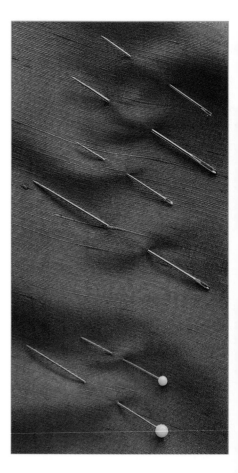

Needles and pins are available in a variety of sizes and styles. Look for rustproof needles and pins made of brass, nickel-plated steel, or stainless steel. Pictured from top to bottom:

Sharps are all-purpose, medium-length needles designed for general sewing.

Crewels are sharp, large-eyed medium-length needles, designed for embroidery.

Betweens are very short and round-eyed. They are useful for hand quilting and making fine stitches.

Milliner's needles are long with round eyes and are used for making long basting or gathering stitches.

Straight pins are used for general sewing. They should be slim and are usually 1 1/16" (2.7 cm) long. Pins with colored ball heads are easier to see and are less likely to get lost than those with flat heads.

Quilting pins are 1 3/4" (4.5 cm) long. Their extra length makes them ideal for use on bulky fabrics or fabrics with extra loft.

A Thimble protects your finger while hand sewing. Available in a variety of styles and sizes, it is worn on whichever finger you use to push the needle through the fabric. Most people prefer either the middle or ring finger. Using a thimble is an acquired habit. Some people can't get along without one, while others feel they are a nuisance.

B Pincushion provides a safe and handy place to store pins. One style is worn on the wrist for convenience. Another style, a magnetic tray, attracts and holds steel pins. Be careful not to place any magnetic tools near a computerized machine, because the magnet may interfere with the machine's memory.

C Needle threader eases threading of hand and machine needles. This is especially useful if you have difficulty seeing something that small.

D Beeswax with holder strengthens thread and prevents tangling while hand sewing.

Measuring & Marking Tools

A Transparent ruler allows you to see what you are measuring and marking. It also is used to check fabric grainline.

B Yardstick (meterstick) should be made of smooth hardwood or metal.

C Tape measure has the flexibility helpful for taking body measurements. Select one made of a material that will not stretch.

D Seam gauge is a 6" (15 cm) metal or plastic ruler with a sliding marker. It helps make quick, accurate measurements and can be used to measure seam allowance widths.

E Marking chalk is available in several forms: as powder in a rolling wheel dispenser, as a pencil, or as a flat slice. Chalk lines are easily removable from most fabrics.

F Fabric marking pens are available in both air-erasable and water-erasable forms. Air-erasable marks disappear within 48 hours; water-erasable marks wash off with a sprinkling of water.

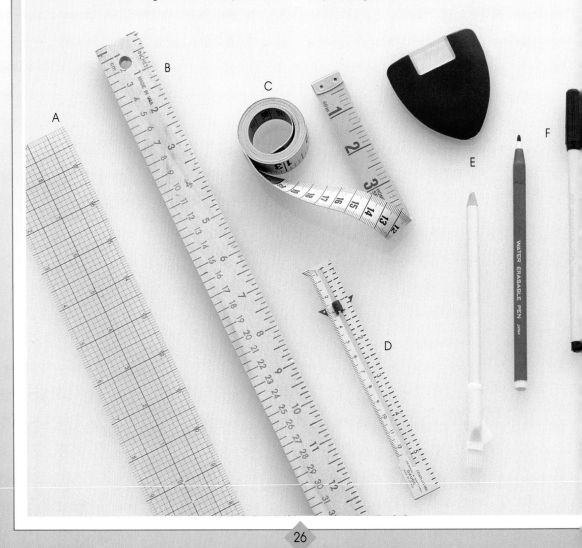

Cutting Tools

Buy quality cutting tools and use them only for your sewing! Cutting paper or other household materials will dull your cutting tools quickly. Dull tools are not only tiresome to work with, they can also damage fabric. Scissors have both handles the same size; shears have one handle larger than the other. The best-quality scissors and shears are hot-forged, high-grade steel, honed to a fine cutting edge. Have your cutting tools sharpened periodically by a qualified professional.

G Bent-handled dressmaker's shears are best for cutting out garment pieces because the angle of the lower blade lets fabric lie flat on the cutting surface. Blade lengths of 7" or 8" (18 or 20.5 cm) are most popular, but lengths of up to 12" (30.5 cm) are available. Select a blade length appropriate for the size of your hand; shorter lengths for smaller hands. Left-handed models are also available. If you intend to sew a great deal, invest in a pair of all-steel, chrome-plated shears for heavy-duty cutting. Lighter models with stainless steel blades and plastic handles are fine for less-frequent sewing or lightweight fabrics.

H Sewing scissors with pointed tips are handy for clipping threads and trimming and clipping seam allowances. A 6" (15 cm) blade is suitable for most tasks.

I Seam ripper quickly removes stitches and opens buttonholes. Use it carefully to avoid cutting the fabric.

J Rotary cutter works like a pizza cutter and can be used by left-handed or right-handed sewers. A locking mechanism retracts the blade for safety. Use the rotary cutter with a special plastic mat.

K Cutting mat must be used with the rotary cutter. It is available in different sizes, with or without grid lines. The self-healing mat protects both the work surface and the blade.

L Pinking shears and pinking rotary cutters are used to finish seams. They cut fabric in a zigzag or scalloped pattern instead of a straight line.

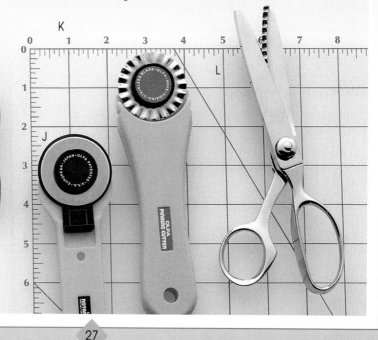

Pressing Tools

Pressing at each stage of construction is the secret to a perfectly finished garment. The general rule is to press each stitched seam before crossing it with another.

A Steam/spray iron should have a wide temperature range to accommodate all fabrics. Buy a dependable, name-brand iron. An iron that steams and sprays at any setting, not just the higher heat settings, is helpful for fabrics with synthetic fibers.

B Press cloth helps prevent iron shine and is always used when applying fusibles. The transparent cloth allows you to see if the fabric is smooth and the layers are properly aligned.

C Teflon™-coated sole plate guard, available to fit most irons, eliminates the need for a press cloth.

A

B

D

D Seam roll is a firmly packed cylindrical cushion for pressing seams. The bulk of the fabric falls to the sides away from the iron, preventing the seam from making an imprint on the right side of the fabric.

E Pressing ham is a firmly packed cushion for pressing curved areas of a garment.

F Sleeve board looks like two small ironing boards attached one on top of the other. It is useful for pressing sleeves one layer at a time to avoid unwanted creases.

C

E

F

Special Products

Many special products and gadgets are designed to save time in various steps of the sewing process. Just as you consider and invest in timesaving devices for other aspects of your life, consider and buy these aids according to your sewing needs. The more you sew, the more these products will become a necessity.

Before using a new product, read the instructions carefully. Learn what special handling or care is required, and for what fabrics or techniques it is suited. Here are some specialized products that you may find helpful for sewing clothes.

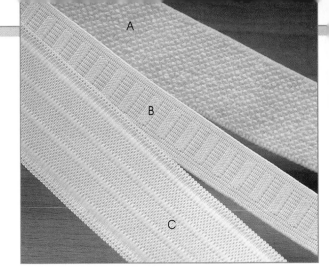

Elastics can be purchased in a variety of widths and styles, either in precut packages or by the yard (meter). Softer elastics **(A)** are suitable for pajamas or boxer shorts; nonroll elastic **(B)** stays flat in the casing; some wide elastic has channels for topstitching **(C)**.

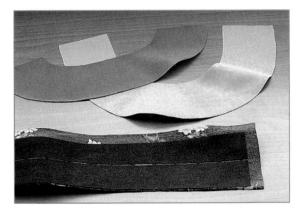

Interfacing plays a supporting role in almost every garment. It is an inner layer of fabric, used to stabilize the fabric in areas like necklines and waistbands, or give support behind buttons and buttonholes. Interfacings may be woven, nonwoven, or knit; the easiest forms to use are heat fusible.

Bodkin is used to thread elastic through a casing. One end holds the elastic tightly while you feed the tool through the narrow casing.

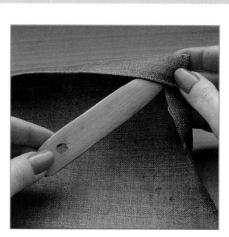

Hook and loop tape. One of the greatest inventions ever, hook and loop tape is useful in many situations for holding things together. For instance, hook and loop tape works well for holding removable shoulder pads in place.

Point turner is helpful for perfecting corners, such as at the top of a pocket or at the ends of a waistband. Slip the tool inside the garment, and gently poke the fabric out into a point.

Cutting boards protect table finishes from scratches. Available in cardboard, plastic, or padded styles, these boards also hold fabric more securely while cutting. Square off fabric using the marked lines, and use the 1" (2.5 cm) squares as an instant measure.

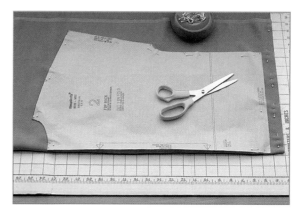

Liquid fray preventer is a colorless plastic liquid that prevents fraying by stiffening the fabric slightly. It is helpful when you have clipped too far into a seam allowance or want to reinforce a buttonhole. It may discolor some fabrics, so test before using, and apply carefully. The liquid may be removed with rubbing alcohol. It dries to a permanent finish that will withstand laundering and dry cleaning.

Fabric Information

The instructions for each individual project in this book offer advice about types of fabric to use. However, the range of possible fabrics for many projects will still involve decision making on your part. It will be helpful to learn as much as you can about fabrics by reading this section. Then browse through fabric stores, handling the fabrics and reading the content and care information at the end of the fabric bolts.

You might already know that you want a solid or print fabric in a certain color, or that you want a dressy or casual look to a finished garment. You'll also want to consider the ease of care. Are you content with a garment that will require dry cleaning or ironing? Would you prefer to build a wash-and-wear wardrobe?

Types of Fabrics

Natural fabrics are made from plant or animal fibers, spun into yarns: cotton, wool, silk, and linen are most common. Naturals are often considered the easiest fabrics to sew. Synthetic fabrics, made from chemically produced fibers, include nylon, acrylic, acetate, and polyester. Synthetic fabrics are made to resemble the look and feel of natural fabrics. Polyester may look like cotton or silk, acetate and nylon shimmer like silk, and acrylic mimics the texture and appearance of wool. Rayon is a man-made fiber made from a plant source. Each fiber has unique characteristics, desirable for different reasons. Many fabrics are a blend of natural and synthetic fibers, offering you the best qualities of each, such as the breathable comfort of cotton blended with the wrinkle resistance of polyester.

Silk

Cotton

Linen

Wool

Polyester

Rayon

Nylon

Acetate

Acrylic

More About
Fabric

Woven Fabrics

Woven fabrics have straight lengthwise and crosswise yarns. The pattern in which the yarns are woven gives the fabric its characteristic surface texture and appearance. The outer edges of woven fabrics are called **SELVAGES.** As a general rule, they should be trimmed away because they are often heavier than the rest of the fabric, and they may shrink when laundered or pressed. Grainlines are the directions in which the fabric yarns run. Strong, stable lengthwise yarns, running parallel to the selvages, form the **LENGTH- WISE GRAIN.** The **CROSSWISE GRAIN** is perpendicular to the lengthwise grain and has a small amount of give. Any diagonal direction, called the **BIAS,** has a fair amount of stretch.

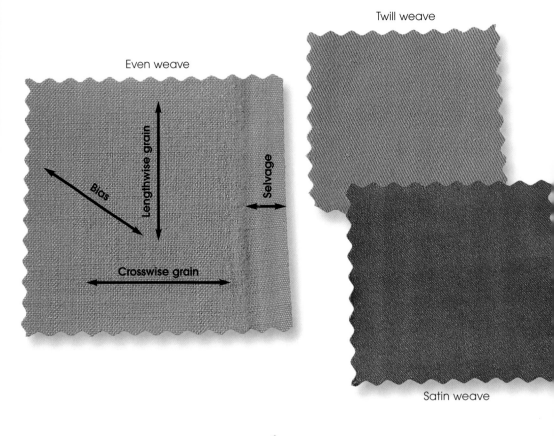

Twill weave

Even weave

Bias

Lengthwise grain

Selvage

Crosswise grain

Satin weave

Knit Fabrics

Knit fabrics consist of rows of interlocking loops of yarn, as in a hand-knit sweater, but usually on a finer scale. Knit fabrics are more flexible than other fabrics, and they all stretch. These features mean that garments made of knits require less fitting and offer more freedom of movement. When sewing with knits, select patterns that are specifically designed for knit fabrics.

Knit fabric is made from interlocking looped stitches. The lengthwise rows of stitches are called **RIBS;** the crosswise rows are called **COURSES.** These ribs and courses correspond to the lengthwise and crosswise grains of woven fabrics.

Patterns designed for knit fabrics have a stretch gauge. Fold over the fabric along a crosswise course several inches (centimeters) from a cut end, and test its degree of stretch against the gauge. If the fabric stretches the necessary amount without distortion, it is suitable for the pattern.

Stretch terry

Synthetic fleece

Double knit

Sweatshirt fleece

Novelty knit

Even More About
Fabric

Fabrics in a store are divided into fashion fabrics and decorator fabrics. Fashion fabrics, designed for sewing clothes, are usually folded double and rolled on cardboard bolts. They vary in crosswise width; the most common are 36", 45", and 60" (91.5, 115, and 152.5 cm). Decorator fabrics are generally not suitable for sewing clothes; they are designed for sewing pillows, window treatments, and slipcovers. Most have stain-resistant finishes, and are rolled on tubes. However, you may select a lightweight tapestry fabric, for instance, for a unique vest.

Most stores arrange their fashion fabrics according to the fiber content or fabric style. For instance, all the wools and wool blends, suitable for skirts, pants, vests, and jackets, may be found together in one area of the store. The bridal and special-occasion fabrics are located in another area. Knits are also often grouped together. It's fun to just browse and visualize how different fabrics will look made into garments. Most fabric stores provide mirrors so that you can hold a fabric in front of you and judge the effects of its color and design.

Fabric Preparation

Every bolt or roll of fabric should carry a fabric identification label, which tells you its fiber content, width, and care method. All of this information is essential to your selection. Preshrink washable fabrics before cutting the pattern pieces. Wash and dry fabrics the same way you intend to care for the finished garment. Preshrink fabrics that must be dry-cleaned by pressing with steam, moving the iron evenly along the grainlines. Allow the fabric to dry before moving it.

Selecting a
Pattern

Major pattern companies follow a uniform sizing based on standard body measurements. This is not exactly the same as ready-to-wear sizing.

Determining Size

To select the right pattern size, first take your standard body measurements. Wear your usual undergarments and use a tape measure that doesn't stretch. It may be easier to have another person measure you. Record your measurements and compare them with the size chart on the back of the pattern or in the back of the pattern book.

Taking Standard Body Measurements

1 Waistline. Tie a string or piece of elastic around your middle, and allow it to roll to your natural waistline. Measure at this exact location with a tape measure. Leave the string in place as a reference for measuring your hips and back waist length.

2 Hips. Measure around the fullest part of your hips. This is usually 7" to 9" (18 to 23 cm) below the waistline, depending on your height.

3 Bust. Place the tape measure under your arms, across the widest part of the back and the fullest part of the bustline.

4 Back waist length. Measure from the middle of the most prominent bone at the base of the neck down to the waistline string.

Pattern Selection

Selecting a pattern for a garment allows for more creativity than shopping from a ready-to-wear catalog. Pattern catalogs don't limit you to certain fabric, colors, skirt lengths, or types of trims shown on the pages. You are free to choose a combination of features that best reflect your style and are most flattering to you.

Major pattern companies publish new catalogs with each season, which means that designer trends seen in clothing stores are reflected in the newest pattern catalogs along with more classic styles. You'll find simple patterns for sewers who prefer the quick and easy styles, and more detailed patterns for experienced sewers. The number of pattern pieces listed on the back of the pattern will provide a clue to the complexity of the pattern. The fewer pieces, the easier the project. Also, the pattern may indicate whether it is intended for knits only.

Pattern catalogs are usually divided into categories by garment types and marked by index tabs. The newest fashions often appear in the first few pages of each category. Pattern illustrations are accompanied by information on recommended fabrics and yardage requirements. An index at the back of the catalog lists patterns in numerical order along with their page numbers. The back of the catalog also includes a complete size chart for every figure type.

All About
Patterns

The pattern envelope is a selling tool and an educational device. The front generally has a photograph of the finished garment and several drawings of the variations that can be sewn using the pattern. On the pattern back, you'll find detailed information to help you select fabric and all the notions necessary to complete your project.

The Envelope Front

Pattern company name, and style number that corresponds to the number in the catalog, are displayed prominently.

Photograph or fashion illustration shows the main pattern design made up in suitable fabrics. It also indicates how closely or loosely the pattern is intended to fit.

Views, labeled with letters, are alternate designs that can be sewn using the pattern. They may include variations in length, fullness, or other design details.

Size or sizes included in the pattern are indicated near the number. Most patterns include several sizes.

Easy McCALL'S

9422

Size
Small (8,10)
Talla

Taille
Petite

Cont. Un Patron de Costura
Pattern/Patron

PETITE-ABLE®
OVERLOCK/
SERGER TIPS™
SELECT-A-SIZE®

Labels may indicate special considerations: that a pattern is suitable for knits only, is easy to sew, has special fitting or size-related information.

Fabric amounts required for each view in all the available sizes are listed in a chart. Locate the style view and the fabric width at the left; match it with your size at the top. The number where the two columns meet is the amount of fabric you need to buy. **INTERFACING** and elastic requirements are also listed. Metric equivalents are given in a separate chart.

Descriptions of the garment include its style, how it is intended to fit, and construction information for each of the views.

Body measurements and size chart help you determine which size to select and follow in the pattern. Compare your measurements (page 38) with those in the chart.

Style number is repeated on the pattern back.

Notions, such as thread, buttons, and zippers, are listed in another paragraph.

Number of pattern pieces gives you an idea of how easy or complicated the pattern is to sew.

Fabrics recommended for sewing the garments are listed to help you make your selections. This paragraph will also tell you if certain fabrics are unsuitable, such as stripes or one-way designs.

Back views show the details and style of the back of the garments.

Inside the
Pattern

Even if you love a good puzzle,
your first peek at the pattern
innards can be scary.
Here's what to expect.

You'll find...

Detailed sketches
show you both
front and back
of each view.

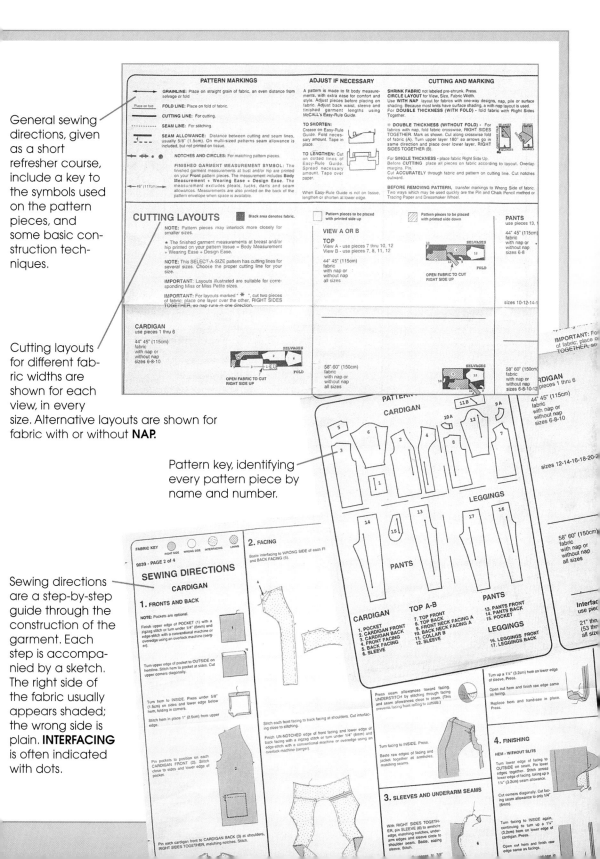

General sewing directions, given as a short refresher course, include a key to the symbols used on the pattern pieces, and some basic construction techniques.

Cutting layouts for different fabric widths are shown for each view, in every size. Alternative layouts are shown for fabric with or without **NAP.**

Pattern key, identifying every pattern piece by name and number.

Sewing directions are a step-by-step guide through the construction of the garment. Each step is accompanied by a sketch. The right side of the fabric usually appears shaded; the wrong side is plain. **INTERFACING** is often indicated with dots.

Pattern Layout

All pattern companies use a universal system of symbols on their pattern pieces. These symbols help you lay out the pattern, show you where to cut, help you match up seamlines, show you where to sew, and give placement guides for things like buttons, buttonholes, and hems. Along with the symbols, you will also find essential instructions printed on the pattern pieces.

Foldline. Often indicated by a long bracket with arrows at each end, it may have "place on fold" instructions. Place the pattern piece with the foldline exactly on the fold of the fabric.

Dots (large and small), squares, or triangles found along the seamlines indicate areas of construction where precise matching, clipping, or stitching is essential.

Grainline.
Heavy solid line with arrows at each end. Place the pattern piece on the fabric with the grainline running parallel to the **SELVAGE.**

Adjustment line.
Double line indicating where the pattern can be lengthened or shortened before cutting out the fabric. If an alteration is necessary, cut the pattern on the double line; spread evenly to lengthen, or overlap evenly to shorten.

Seamlines. Long, broken line, usually 5⁄8″ (1.5 cm) inside the cutting line. Multisize patterns often do not have seamlines printed on them.

Cutting line. Heavy solid line along the outer edge of the pattern, often shown with a scissors symbol. Cut on this line. When more than one size is printed on one pattern, the cutting lines may be various styles of solid, dotted, or dashed lines, to help you distinguish one size from the next.

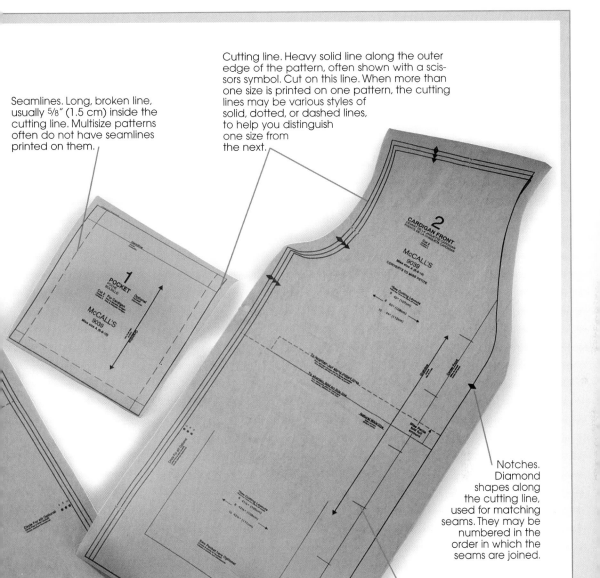

Notches. Diamond shapes along the cutting line, used for matching seams. They may be numbered in the order in which the seams are joined.

Button and buttonhole placement marks. Solid lines indicate the length of the buttonhole, if you are using the button size suggested on the pattern back. "X" or a button symbol shows the button size and placement.

Hemline. Hem allowance is printed on the cutting line. Turn the hem up the specified amount, adjusting as necessary.

Detail positions. Broken or solid lines indicating the placement for pockets or other details. Mark the position for accurate placement.

continued

Prepare a large work area, such as a dining room table covered with a cutting board (page 31). Assemble all the pattern pieces you will be needing, and press out any wrinkles with a warm, dry iron.

Locate and circle the correct pattern layout diagram (page 43) on your pattern guide sheet. These diagrams usually show you the easiest, most efficient way to lay out your pattern. Some fabrics have a **NAP**, meaning they have definite up and down directions. For these fabrics, pattern pieces must all be laid out in the same direction.

Fold the fabric in half, lengthwise. Smooth it out on the work surface, so that the **SELVAGES** align and the **CROSSWISE GRAIN** is perpendicular to them. Arrange the pattern pieces as indicated in the layout diagram. White pattern shapes indicate the piece is to be placed with the printed side up. Shaded pieces are to be placed with the printed side down. Be sure to follow any other incidental directions that pertain to your layout. After all the pieces are in place, pin them to the fabric. Do not begin cutting until all the pattern pieces are in place.

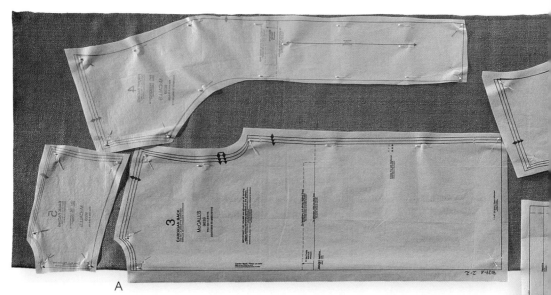

A

Pinning

A First, position the pattern pieces that are to be cut on the fold. Place each one directly on the folded edge of the fabric. Pin the corners diagonally. Then continue pinning near the outer edge, placing the pins parallel to the cutting line. Space the pins about 3" (7.5 cm) apart; closer together on curves.

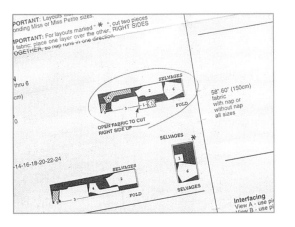

Quick Reference

Fold the fabric in half, lengthwise.

When your fabric is folded like this, you will end up with mirror-image pieces for the left and right sides of the garment. Pattern directions usually suggest folding right sides together. Sometimes there are advantages to folding wrong sides together, such as having a better view of the fabric design or ease in marking. Either way will work.

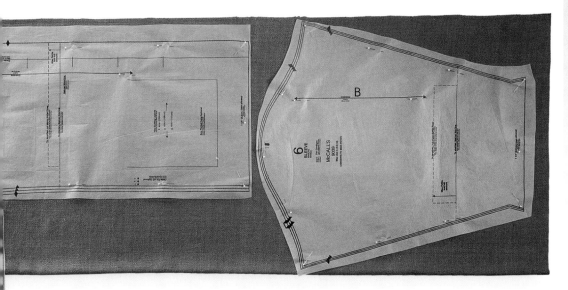

B Place the straight-grain pattern pieces on the fabric, with the grain-line arrow parallel to the selvages on woven fabrics or parallel to the **RIBS** on knits. Measure from each end of the arrow to the selvage, shifting the pattern until the distances are equal. Pin both ends of the grainline so the pattern will not shift. Then pin the outer edges.

Cutting & Marking

Don't be intimidated! Locate the correct cutting lines, and cut with confidence. Transfer the necessary marks, and you'll be ready to sew!

Cutting

Accuracy is important, since mistakes made in cutting cannot always be corrected. Before cutting, double-check the placement of the pattern pieces.

Using bent-handled shears, cut with long, firm strokes, cutting directly on the cutting line. Take shorter strokes around curves. If you are using a multisize pattern, be sure that you follow the correct cutting line all the time.

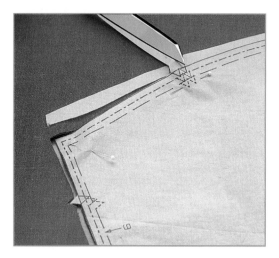

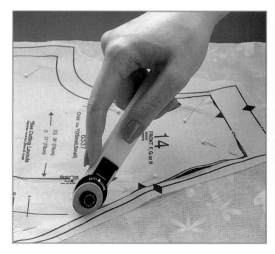

Notches can be cut outward, especially if the fabric is loosely woven or if the pattern calls for 1/4" (6 mm) **SEAM ALLOWANCES.** Cut multiple notches as one unit, not separately. Or, you can cut directly through the notches, and then mark them with short snips into the seam allowances.

If you prefer to use a **ROTARY CUTTER AND MAT,** be sure to keep the mat under the area being cut. Use steady, even pressure, and, above all, keep fingers and small children away from the rotary cutter.

Marking

Keep the pattern pieces pinned in place after cutting. Transfer pattern symbols to the appropriate side of the fabric, using one of the following methods.

Pins are a quick way to transfer marks. Since they may fall out easily, use pin marks only when you intend to sew immediately. Or, pin-mark first, remove the pattern, and mark again, using chalk or erasable fabric marker.

Erasable fabric markers are felt-tip pens designed specifically for sewing needs. Air-erasable marks disappear within 48 hours. Water-erasable marks disappear with a spritz of water.

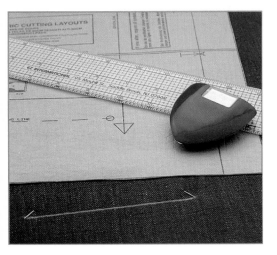

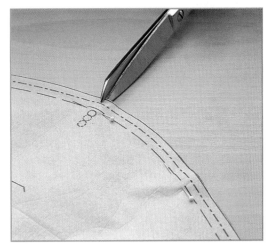

Chalk is available in pencil form or as a powder in a rolling-wheel dispenser.

Snips are handy for marking things like dots at shoulder seams. Make shallow snips into the seam allowances at the dot locations.

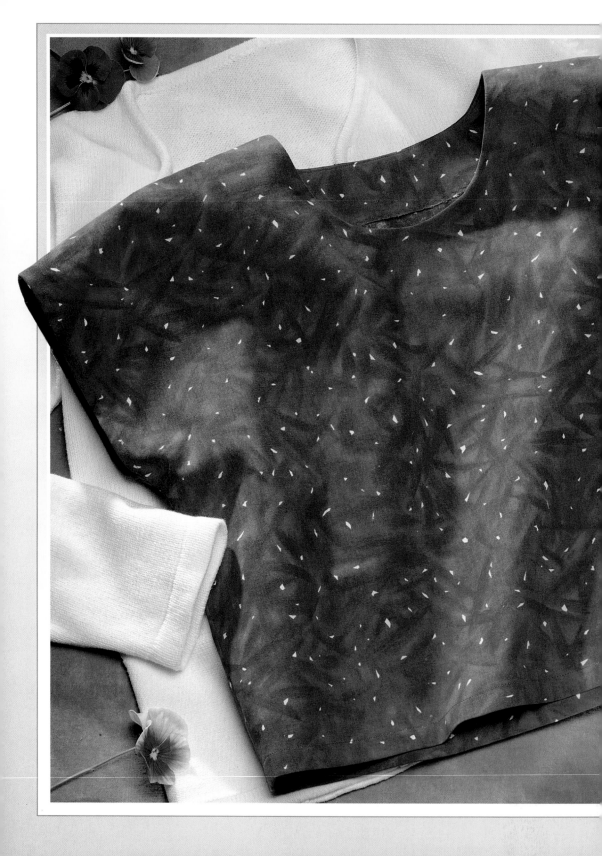

Simple *Shells*

A simple shell is a great starter project for a beginning sewer. Consider making several in a variety of fabrics and colors to wear alone or under blazers or cardigan sweaters. Shells can be plain or enhanced with side slits, shoulder pads, or **TOPSTITCHING.**

Select a plain blouse pattern with a rounded neckline that has just four pieces: front, back, front neck **FACING,** and back neck facing. Relatively lightweight woven fabrics, such as cotton, linen, or rayon, are easiest to work with. As a beginner, you might want to avoid stripes or plaids that would require matching at the side or shoulder seams. Allover prints, very narrow vertical stripes, or plain colors are good choices.

WHAT YOU'LL LEARN

How to sew **SEAMS**

How to **FINISH** seams

How to sew a neck facing

How to apply fusible **INTERFACING**

How to stitch a hem by machine

WHAT YOU'LL NEED

Shell pattern

Woven fabric
(check pattern for amount)

Matching all-purpose thread

Lightweight, fusible interfacing (check pattern for amount)

Let's Begin

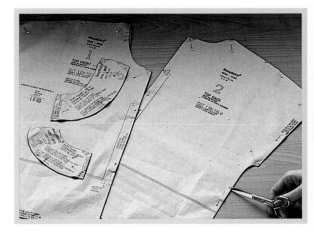

1 Prepare the fabric (page 37), lay out the pattern (page 44), and cut the fabric (page 48). Transfer any necessary marks (page 49). Set your sewing machine on a straight stitch of 10 to 12 stitches per inch, which equals 2 to 2.5 mm. For most fabrics, a universal machine needle size 12/80 will work fine.

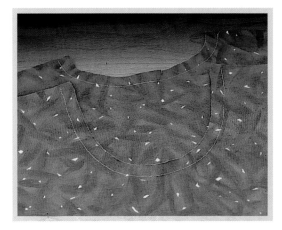

2 **Staystitch** 1/2" (1.3 cm) from the cut edge of the neckline on both the front and back shell sections. Starting from a shoulder, sew to a point just past the center of the shell. Then repeat from the opposite shoulder, overlapping the first stitches about 1/2" (1.3 cm). Be careful not to pull and stretch the fabric as you go.

3 Place the front over the back, right sides together, aligning the cut edges of the shoulder seams and matching notches. Insert pins along the shoulders, perpendicular to the cut edges.

Quick Reference

Staystitch. Stitch a line about 1/2" (1.3 cm) from the fabric edge before sewing garment pieces together. Staystitching is recommended for curved or **BIAS** edges; it prevents the fabric from stretching.

4 Place the fabric under the presser foot, with the front facing up. Stitch 5/8" (1.5 cm) seams, **backstitching (p. 17)** at the beginning and end of each seam. Remove the pins as you come to them.

TIP: Avoid the temptation to sew over pins! You risk scratching the presser foot, dulling or breaking the sewing machine needle, or causing more severe mechanical problems.

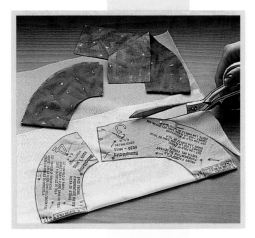

5 Finish the **SEAM ALLOWANCES** (page 19). **PRESS** the seams flat; then open the seam allowances and press them again, moving the iron along the center of the seam.

6 Cut interfacing, using the pattern pieces for the front and back neck facings. Follow the pattern instructions for laying out the pieces.

TIP: The practice of pressing the seam flat first before pressing it open sets the stitches in the seamline and ultimately makes a better-looking seam.

continued

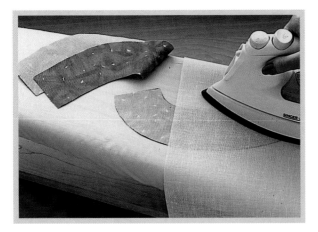

continued

7 Place the front and back neck facing pieces wrong side up on the ironing board. Place the corresponding interfacing pieces on top of the fabric pieces with fusible side down. Cover with a **press cloth. Follow the manufacturer's directions** for fusing the interfacing. Lift and move the iron as needed to cover the entire facing.

8 Place the front neck facing over the back neck facing, right sides together, aligning the cut edges of the shoulder seams. Insert pins along the shoulder seams, perpendicular to the cut edges.

9 Place the facings under the presser foot. Stitch 5/8" (1.5 cm) seams, backstitching at the beginning and end of each seam. Remove the pins as you come to them. Finish the seam allowances. Press the seams flat; then press them open.

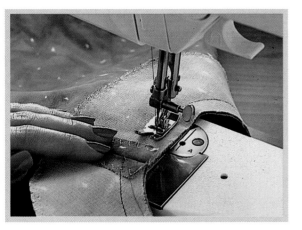

Press cloth. Using a press cloth will prevent any stray fusible substance from collecting on the bottom of your iron.

Follow the manufacturer's directions. The interfacing bolt is wrapped with a long sheet of plastic on which the directions are printed. Have the store clerk cut off a section of the directions for you to take home.

10 Finish the outside raw edge of the facing. Placing right sides of the fabric together, pin the facing to the neckline; match up the shoulder seams and any notches. Sew around the entire neck edge using a ⁵⁄₈" (1.5 cm) seam allowance, overlapping the seamline by several stitches as you complete the circle. Keep the shoulder seam allowances open flat.

11 Trim the shell neckline seam allowance to ¼" (6 mm); trim the facing seam allowance to ⅛" (3 mm). This step, called **GRADING,** reduces bulk. **CLIP** into the neckline seam allowance every ½" (1.3 cm), clipping up to, but not through, the stitches. Clipping allows the facing to turn smoothly to the inside and lie flat.

12 Place the facing **(A)** under the presser foot, so the needle is aligned to enter the fabric just to the right of the seam; the shell **(B)** extends off the left of the machine bed. Turn the seam allowance toward the right so it is tucked under the facing. Stitch all around the neckline very close to the neck seam, keeping the seam allowance turned toward the facing. You will be stitching through the facing and the seam allowance, but not through the shell. This step, called **UNDERSTITCHING,** helps the facing lie flat.

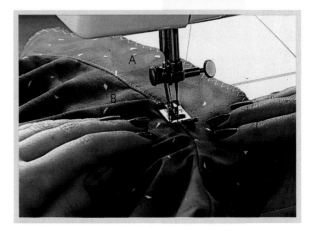

continued

continued

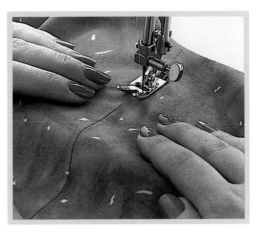

13 Turn the facing to the inside of the shell, and press. You will notice that the seam rolls slightly to the inside of the shell. Align the shoulder seams. ***Stitch in the ditch*** of the seams to keep the facings in place.

14 Turn under the **hem allowance** at the armhole openings; press. Then unfold the pressed edge, and turn the cut edge under, aligning it to the pressed fold-line. Press the outer fold. Refold the hem, enclosing the cut edge; pin.

15 Stitch along the inner folded edge of the hem; remove the pins as you come to them. Your pattern may direct you to sew side seams before armhole hems. Our method seems easier for this style top.

Stitch in the ditch. Using short stitches, stitch directly into the well of the seam. Your stitches will practically disappear.

Hem allowance. The pattern has already allowed extra length for turning under and finishing the armhole openings and the lower edge. This amount is indicated on your pattern.

16 Turn the shell inside out. Line up the raw edges of the front and back side seams, matching the notches. Pin them together, inserting the pins perpendicular to the edges. Sew a ⅝" (1.5 cm) seam down each side, backstitching at the beginning and end of the seams.

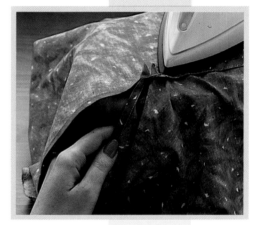

17 Finish the seam allowances. Clip along the curved underarm portion of the seam every ½" (1.3 cm) or so to ensure that it will lie smooth when turned. Press the seam flat; then press it open.

18 Hem the lower edge of the shell as for the armhole opening, following steps 14 and 15.

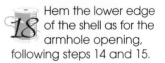

You're finished, and wasn't that easy? Shells are great for expanding your wardrobe in a hurry!

Shell VARIATIONS

Your pattern may have a different neckline than the one on page 50. Other styles may feature a V-neckline or a square neckline. In both cases, you will need to clip up to, but not through, the stitching at the corner before you trim in step 11.

TOPSTITCHING is a popular detail for shell necklines. Pin through the shell and facing, inserting the pins perpendicular to the stitching line. From the right side of the garment, sew a straight stitch, removing pins as you come to them. Place tape on the machine bed as a guide.

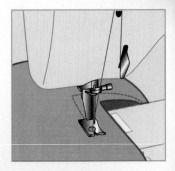

Removable shoulder pads can be secured inside your shell with hook and loop tape (page 31). Try on the shell, and pin the shoulder pads in place. Hand-stitch short lengths of soft loop tape to the shoulder seam allowances. Then stitch hook tape to the shoulder pads.

Inside view for pad positioning

In some patterns, the side seams are open at the bottom, allowing more freedom of movement. Turn under, press, and pin the seam allowances of the open ends in the same manner as for the sleeve and bottom hems. Stitch the bottom hem and side slits in one continuous stitching line, pivoting at the corners.

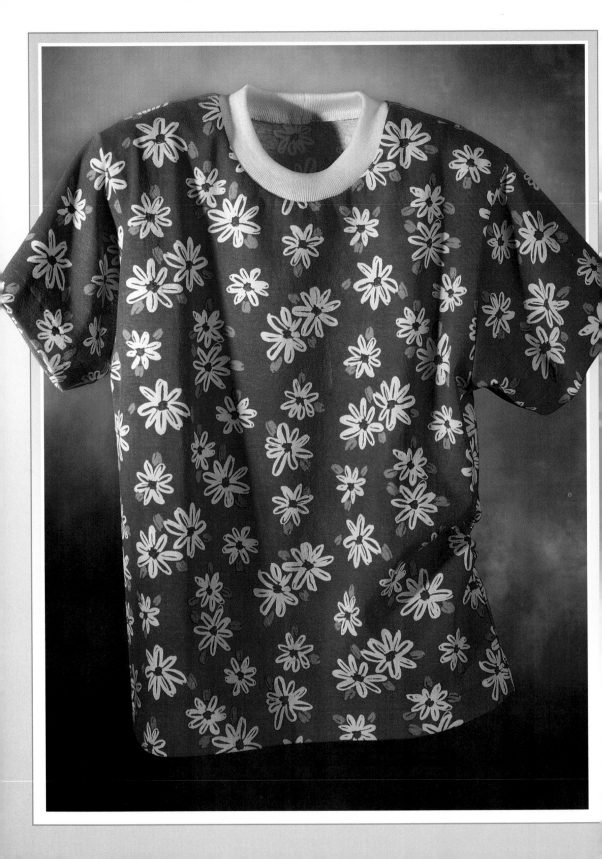

T-shirts

T-shirts are classic and versatile; it seems you can never have too many. As you become more experienced, you'll be surprised how quickly you are able to make them. The fun begins in selecting your knit fabric (page 35) from the array of stripes, prints, and colorful solids available.

To help you decide which pattern to buy, note the way the T-shirts fit the models or sketches on the package front. Some patterns are designed for an "oversized" look, others are meant to fit the form of your body more closely. Your pattern should have four pieces: front, back, sleeve, and neck **RIBBING.** Some may also have a piece for sleeve ribbing.

The fit of the T-shirt will vary with the fabric's degree of stretch. T-shirt patterns, designed for knits only, indicate the amount of stretch required of the fabric. For instance, "25% stretch crosswise" would indicate that 4" (10 cm) of fabric will stretch on the **CROSSWISE GRAIN** an additional 1" (2.5 cm). Always test the degree of stretch in the fabric, especially if you are making a close-fitting T-shirt.

WHAT YOU'LL LEARN	WHAT YOU'LL NEED
Techniques for sewing with knits	T-shirt pattern (designed for stretch knits)
How to sew in sleeves	Knit fabric (check pattern for amount)
How to apply ribbing to a neckline	Scraps of fusible **INTERFACING**
	Ribbing (check pattern for amount)
	Matching all-purpose thread

Let's Begin

1 Prepare the fabric (page 37); however, don't wash the ribbing, as the raw edges are likely to stretch out of shape. T-shirts are easiest to sew using **1/4" (6 mm) seam allowances.** If your pattern pieces have 5/8" (1.5 cm) **SEAM ALLOWANCES,** trim them down to 1/4" (6 mm) before laying out the pattern. Lay out the pattern (page 44), and cut the fabric (page 48). Transfer any necessary marks (page 49). Insert a ballpoint sewing machine needle; size 11/70 or 12/80 is suitable for most knits. Cut two 1/2" (1.3 cm) strips of fusible interfacing the length of the shoulder **SEAM.** Place a strip even with the cut edge of each back shoulder, on the wrong side of the fabric. Fuse the strips in place, *following the manufacturer's directions (p. 55).* This is done to *stabilize the shoulder seams.*

2 Place the T-shirt front over the back, right sides together, aligning the shoulder seam allowance edges. Pin, inserting the pins perpendicular to the edges. Stitch the front and back T-shirt sections together at the shoulder seams, using a 1/4" (6 mm) seam allowance; *backstitch (p. 17)* a few stitches at each edge. Since the shoulder seams are stabilized, a straight stitch is appropriate here.

3 Add a second row of machine stitching (either a straight stitch or a narrow zigzag) next to the first row, within the seam allowance. **PRESS** the shoulder seam allowances toward the shirt back.

4 Mark the center front and center back of the neckline with pins. Then bring the two centers together and mark the points halfway between with pins. (These marks should be slightly ahead of the shoulder seams.) The neckline is now divided into fourths.

5 Sew the short ends of the **ribbing, right sides together,** forming a circle. Use 1/4" (6 mm) seam allowance, and sew with a short straight stitch. **Press the seam open with your fingers.**

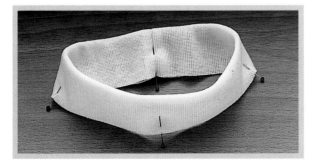

Quick Reference

1/4" (6 mm) seam allowances. Some patterns made especially for knits are designed with 1/4" (6 mm) seam allowances, rather than 5/8" (1.5 cm). In many cases, running the outside edge of the presser foot along the cut edge of the fabric results in a 1/4" (6 mm) seam. Run a test to be sure.

Stabilize the shoulder seams. Shoulder seams follow the crosswise grain, the direction in which knit fabrics stretch the most. However, it is not desirable or necessary to have shoulder seams that stretch. Narrow strips of fusible interfacing help the seams keep their intended length. You'll also find that this makes sewing in the stretchy direction much easier.

Ribbing, right sides together. Sometimes knit fabrics and ribbings do not have a right or wrong side. To test, gently stretch the raw edge on the crosswise grain of the ribbing. If the edge curls to one side, that side is the right side of the fabric. If it doesn't curl to either side, either side can be used on the outside.

Press the seam open with your fingers. Avoid pressing ribbing with an iron, as this may destroy its elasticity.

6 Fold the ribbing in half, lengthwise, with the raw edges even and the seam allowances on the inside. Divide the ribbing into fourths, as you did the neckline. Mark these sections with pins.

continued

continued

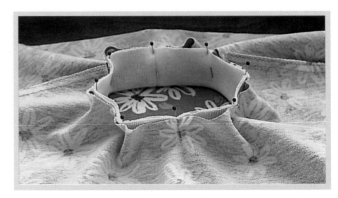

7 Pin the ribbing to the right side of the neckline, aligning the ribbing seam to the center back pin mark; match up the remaining pin marks.

8 Place the fabric under the presser foot, with the ribbing facing up. Stitch with a narrow zigzag or stretch stitch (page 18), keeping the raw edges even and stretching the ribbing evenly to fit each section between pins. Remove the pins as you come to them.

9 Stitch again next to the first row, using a narrow, medium-length zigzag stitch. Gently press the ribbing toward the shirt, being careful not to stretch the ribbing.

10 Make sure you have marked the top of the sleeve and any other notches on the sleeve and shirt as indicated on the pattern pieces. With right sides together, pin the sleeve to the armhole of the shirt, matching the top dot or notch to the shoulder seam, and aligning any other notches. Pin frequently, easing in any extra sleeve fullness.

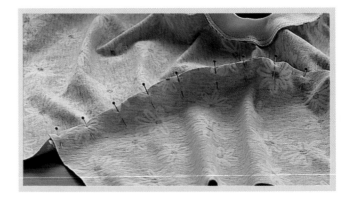

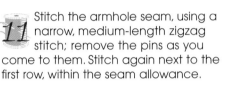
11 Stitch the armhole seam, using a narrow, medium-length zigzag stitch; remove the pins as you come to them. Stitch again next to the first row, within the seam allowance.

12 Repeat steps 10 and 11 for the other sleeve. Press the seams toward the sleeves. With the right sides together, pin the shirt front to the shirt back along the sides and sleeves, matching the underarm seams.

13 Stitch and **FINISH** the seams in the same manner as for the sleeve seams, beginning at the lower edge of the shirt and sewing continuously to the lower edge of the sleeve. Press the seams toward the back.

TIP: You can press the side seams, simply by slipping the shirt over the end of the ironing board. Insert a seam roll or sleeve board (page 29) into the sleeve, so you can press the seam allowance to the side without pressing unwanted creases into the opposite side of the sleeve.

14 Turn under the lower **hem allowance (p. 57)**, as specified by your pattern. Stitch the hem by hand (page 22) or by machine (page 23); select a method that will allow the hem to stretch, if necessary. Hem the lower edges of the sleeves in the same manner.

CHANGE THE
Look

If the neckline slips comfortably over the head, you can use the shirt fabric in place of ribbing. **Topstitch (p. 74)** close to the seam for added detail. Double-needle hems are a perfect finishing touch.

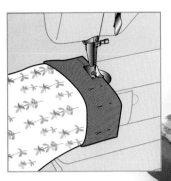

In some patterns, the sleeves may be finished with ribbing. Follow the directions for the neckline ribbing.

Mock turtleneck or turtleneck styles are created with wider ribbing pieces. Ribbing fabric is often dyed to match other knits.

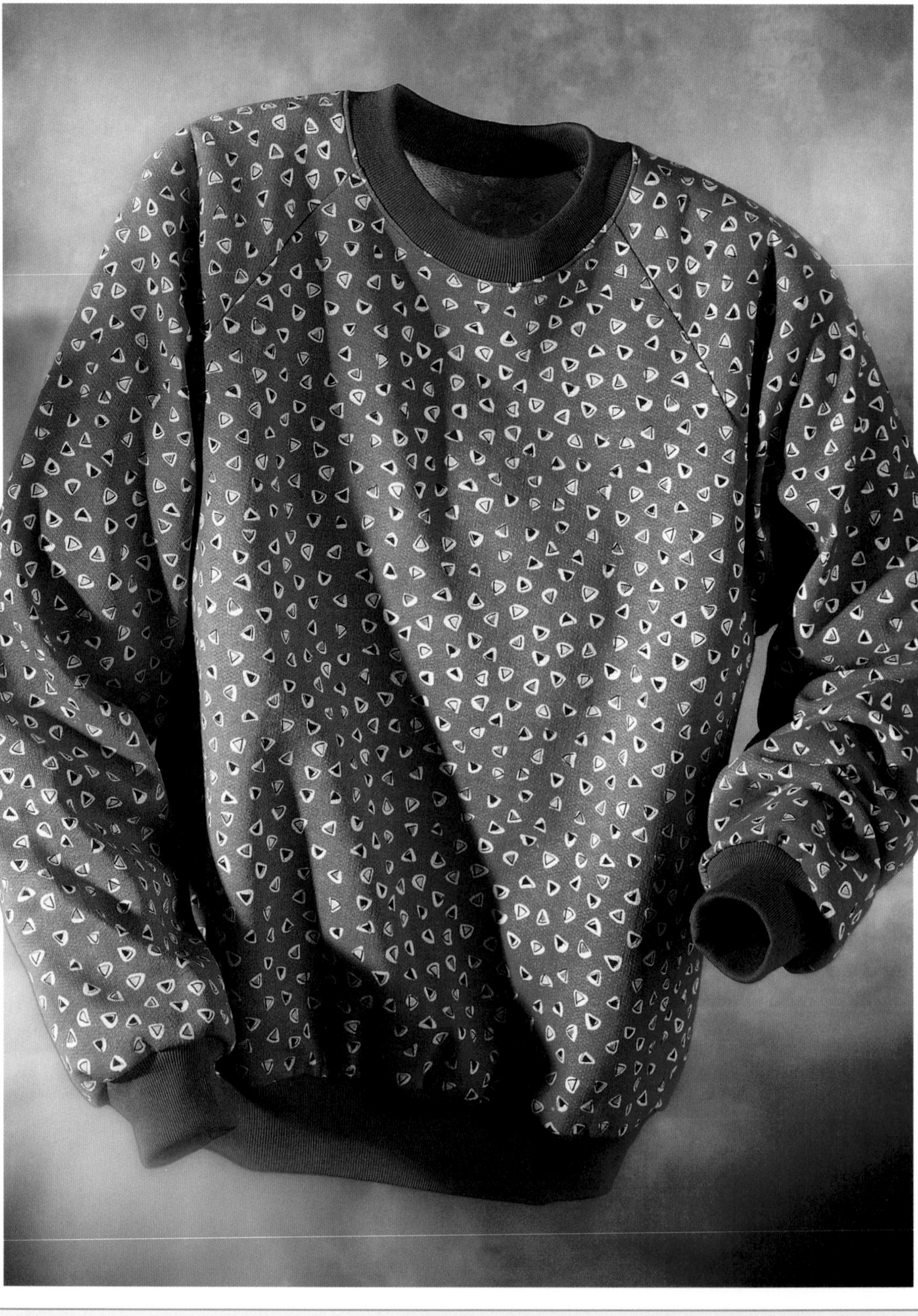

Raglan-sleeve *Sweatshirts*

Perhaps the most popular casual garment ever designed is the sweat-shirt. This particular style features raglan sleeves, which are comfortable to wear and easy to sew. Sweatshirts with **DROP-SHOULDER** styling are sewn following the directions for T-shirts (page 61).

Sweatshirt fleeces are knits, available in acrylic, cotton, and cotton/polyester blend. They tend to have less stretch than other knits, so be sure to select a size that allows plenty of room for a comfortable fit and freedom of movement. Like other knits, today's sweatshirt fleece comes in lots of colors and prints and sometimes in varying textures. Most often, however, the texture is smooth on the right side and soft and fuzzy on the wrong side.

Look for a pattern that has three main pattern pieces: front, back, and sleeve, as well as three **RIBBING** pattern pieces: for the neck, cuffs, and the bottom of the sweatshirt.

WHAT YOU'LL LEARN	WHAT YOU'LL NEED
Techniques for sewing with sweatshirt fleece	Raglan-sleeve sweatshirt pattern
How to sew raglan sleeves	Sweatshirt fleece (check pattern for amount)
How to apply ribbing to cuffs and bottom hems	Ribbing (check pattern for amount)
	Matching all-purpose thread

Let's Begin

1 Prepare the fabric (page 37); however, don't wash the ribbing, as the raw edges are likely to stretch out of shape. Sweatshirts are easiest to sew using **1/4" (6 mm) seam allowances (p. 63).** If your pattern has 5/8" (1.5 cm) **SEAM ALLOWANCES,** trim them down to 1/4" (6 mm) before laying out the pattern. Lay out the pattern (page 44), and cut the fabric (page 48). Transfer any necessary marks (page 49). Insert a ballpoint sewing machine needle; size 11/70 or 12/80 is suitable for most sweatshirt fleece.

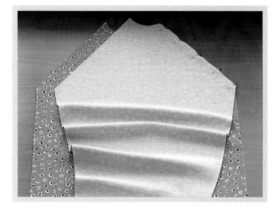

2 Place one sleeve piece over the sweatshirt front, aligning the raw edges and matching the notches. Pin, inserting the pins perpendicular to the edges. This **SEAM** runs from the neckline to the underarm.

TIP: One way to tell the front sleeve seam edge from the back is to count the notches. Front notches usually are single; back notches usually are double.

3 Stitch the seam, using a 1/4" (6 mm) seam allowance; **backstitch (p. 17)** a few stitches at each end. Since sweatshirt fleece doesn't have much stretch to it, a straight stitch is appropriate here.

4 Stitch the other sleeve to the other side of the sweatshirt front. Then stitch the remaining raw edges of the sleeves to opposite sides of the shirt back. You now have a complete circle at the neckline.

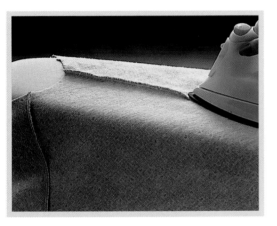

5 Add a second row of machine stitching next to each first row, within the seam allowances (page 18). **PRESS** the front and back seam allowances toward the sleeve.

TIP: If your machine has a stretch overedge stitch (page 18), sew the entire sweatshirt using this stitch. There is no need to finish the seams with a second row of stitching. You'll make sweatshirts twice as fast!

6 With the right sides together, pin the shirt front to the shirt back along the sides and sleeves, matching the sleeve seams.

7 Stitch and **FINISH** the seams in the same manner as for the sleeve seams, beginning at the lower edge of the shirt and sewing continuously to the lower edge of the sleeve. Press the seams toward the back.

continued

continued

8 Mark the center front and center back of the neckline with pins. Then bring the two centers together and mark the points halfway between with pins. The neckline is now divided into fourths.

9 Sew the short ends of the neck **ribbing, right sides together (p. 63)**, forming a circle; sew a 1/4" (6 mm) seam allowance with a short straight stitch. **Press the seam open with your fingers (p. 63).**

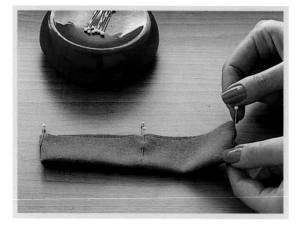

10 Fold the ribbing in half, lengthwise, with the raw edges even and the seam allowances on the inside. Divide the ribbing into fourths, as you did the neckline. Mark these sections with pins.

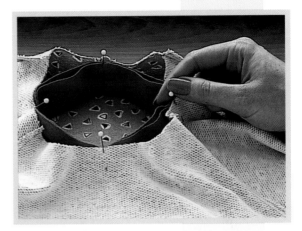

11 Pin the ribbing to the right side of the neckline, aligning the ribbing seam to the center back pin mark. Match up the remaining pin marks.

12 Place the fabric under the presser foot, with the ribbing facing up. Stitch a 1/4" (6 mm) seam with a narrow zigzag or stretch stitch (page 18), keeping the raw edges even and stretching the ribbing to fit each section between pins. Remove the pins as you come to them.

13 Finish the seam allowances together. Gently press the seam allowance toward the shirt, being careful not to stretch the ribbing.

continued

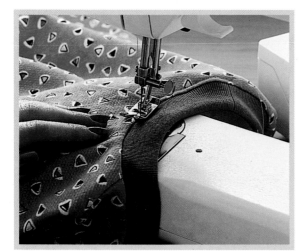

Quick Reference

Topstitch. Stitch along a seam or hem on the right side of a garment to add detail. Topstitching is often 1/8" or 1/4" (3 or 6 mm) away from an edge or a seam.

14 Place the neckline under the presser foot, with the right side facing up. **Topstitch** on the garment 1/8" (3 mm) away from the neckline seam, catching the seam allowance in the stitching.

15 Sew the ribbing to the lower edge and to the end of each sleeve, following the same steps as for the neckline.

TIP: To apply the sleeve ribbing, it is helpful, but not necessary, to use the **FREE ARM** of your sewing machine, if it has one. Slip the sleeve, right side out, onto the free arm, with the ribbing facing up. If your machine does not have a free arm, turn the sleeve inside out, and stitch inside the sleeve cylinder, with the ribbing facing up.

Considering how quickly these sweatshirts go together, you could outfit a whole family in no time!

HAVE FUN WITH
Sweatshirts

Eliminate the bottom rib-
bing, if you prefer, and simply turn up a hem. Before
you cut the fabric, be sure
to allow extra length, including the depth of the hem. A
double-needle hem (page
23) works well here.

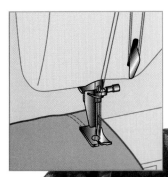

Use your sweatshirt
pattern with other kinds of
knit fabrics, such as a novelty knit,
polar fleece, or stretch terry cloth, to
give you completely different looks.

Pull-on Skirts

Skirts with elastic waistbands are classic, comfortable, and easy-care. Straight or flared versions in varying lengths can be coordinated with a variety of sweaters or other tops for business, dress, or casual wear. Check the pattern envelope for recommended fabrics. Some patterns are designed only for knits and generally fit the body closer, counting on the stretchiness of the fabric to allow you to slide the skirt over your hips. Patterns suitable for woven fabrics will include extra fullness. The first set of directions works for woven or knit fabrics. Alternate steps for sewing with knits begin on page 83. These directions may differ from your pattern; be sure to use the **SEAM ALLOWANCE** given in your pattern.

Select a pattern with two pieces: a front and a back. An elastic **CASING** at the waistline is formed from excess fabric length at the skirt top. The skirt itself may be constructed of two, three, or four sections, depending on whether or not there are center front or back **SEAMS.**

WHAT YOU'LL LEARN

Two methods for sewing
elastic waistlines

Hem alternatives
for skirts

How to sew and **FINISH**
side, front, and back seams

WHAT YOU'LL NEED

Skirt pattern
with elastic waistline

Fabric (check pattern
for amount)

Matching all-purpose thread

1" (2.5 cm) nonroll elastic,
enough to go around
your waist

Let's Begin

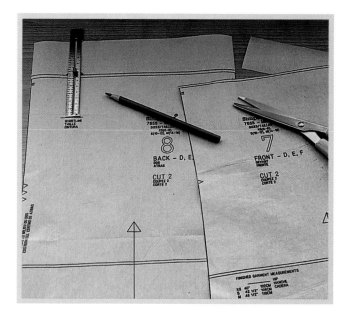

1 To construct the skirt following these directions, 2¾" (7 cm) of fabric must be allowed for the casing above the waistline. This may be different from the casing allowance already on your pattern. Measure this distance from the waistline, and mark a cutting line on your pattern. (Add extra paper, if necessary.) Be sure to mark both front and back pattern pieces.

2 Prepare the fabric (page 37), lay out the pattern (page 44), and cut the fabric (page 48). Transfer any necessary marks (page 49). Insert a size 11/70 or 12/80 sharp or universal sewing machine needle. If your pattern does not have center front or back seams, move on to step 4. If your pattern has a center front seam, place the skirt front pieces right sides together, aligning the center cut edges and matching the notches. Insert pins perpendicular to the center front seam.

TIP: Be sure you are not pinning the pieces together along the side seams. Sometimes it is difficult to tell the difference. Check your pattern to be sure.

Place the fabric under the presser foot with the cut edges aligned to the 5/8″ (1.5 cm) seam allowance guide. Stitch the center front seam, **backstitching (p. 17)** a few stitches at the upper and lower edges. If your pattern has a center back seam, stitch it in the same manner.

TIP: If your skirt has side seam pockets, follow the pattern directions carefully because methods vary greatly.

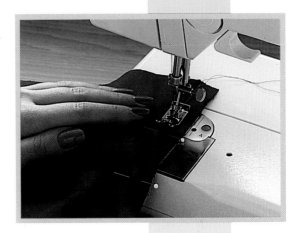

 If it is difficult to tell the skirt front from the back, mark the wrong side of the skirt back, using chalk. Place the front and back skirt pieces right sides together, aligning the side edges and matching the notches. Insert pins perpendicular to the sides. Stitch the side seams, backstitching at the upper and lower edges, and removing pins as you come to them. If you are sewing on a woven fabric, finish (page 19) the edges of all the seam allowances.

PRESS all the seams flat to set the stitching line in the fabric. This may seem unnecessary, but it really does give you a better-looking seam in the end. Then press the seam allowances open.

TIP: To prevent the cut edge of the seam allowance from imprinting the front of the fabric, press seams open over a seam roll or hard cardboard tube.

continued

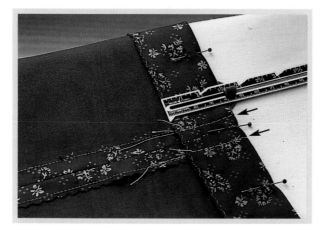

continued

BASTE the seam allowances open flat from the upper edge down about 4" (10 cm) (arrows). This will keep them from getting in the way when you insert the elastic in step 9. Finish the waistline edge, using a multistitch-zigzag (page 19). Fold the upper edge 1 1/2" (3.8 cm) to the wrong side, and press. Insert pins along and perpendicular to the fold.

EDGESTITCH close to the fold around the upper edge of the waistline. Begin and end at a side seam, overlapping the stitches about 1/2" (1.3 cm).

TIP: Sometimes it is difficult to tell the skirt front from the back when the garment is finished. We've sewn a short loop of twill tape under the casing seam to identify the back.

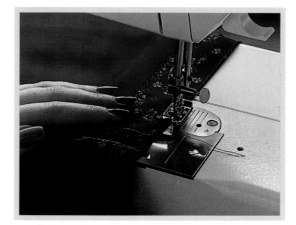

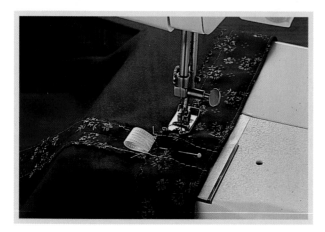

Insert pins along the lower edge of the casing. Place a piece of tape on the bed of your machine 1 1/4" (3.2 cm) from the tip of the needle. Stitch the lower edge of the casing, guiding the upper edge along the tape. Leave a 2" (5 cm) opening at one side seam.

Fasten a safety pin or bodkin (page 30) to one end of the elastic, and insert the elastic through the casing opening. Push and pull the safety pin all the way to the opposite side of the opening. Remove the basting threads from step 6.

TIP: Insert a large safety pin across the free end of the elastic so that it will not get pulled into the opening.

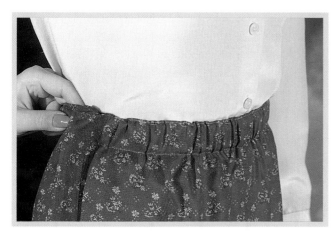

Try on the skirt. Pull up the elastic to fit your waist snugly, yet comfortably; pin the ends together.

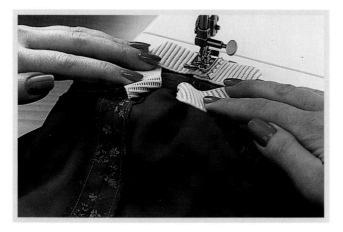

Take off the skirt. Pull the pinned ends of the elastic several inches (centimeters) out of the casing. Trim the overlapped ends to 1/2" (1.3 cm), if necessary. Place them under the presser foot, and stitch through both layers, using a multistitch-zigzag.

continued

continued

12 Machine-stitch the opening in the casing closed. Distribute the casing fullness evenly around the elastic. **Stitch in the ditch (p. 57)** at the seams to keep the elastic from shifting or rolling.

13 Try on the skirt, and have someone **mark the hem length** for you, using chalk or pins.

14 Take off the skirt, and trim the hem allowance to an even depth. (Check the pattern for hem allowance.) Turn under the hem along the markings, and pin. For double-fold hems on slightly flared skirts, it is helpful to hand-baste on the inner fold. Stitch the hem by hand (page 22) or by machine (page 23); select a method that will allow the hem to stretch, if you are using a knit. Give the skirt a final pressing, and give yourself a pat on the back.

Alternate Steps for a Knit Pull-on Skirt

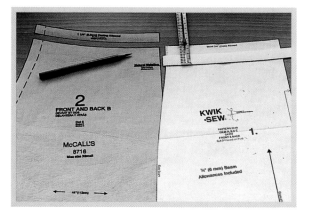

1. To construct a knit skirt following these directions, an amount of fabric equal to **twice the width of the elastic** must be allowed above the waistline. Measure this distance from the waistline, and mark a new cutting line on your pattern. (Add extra paper, if necessary.) Be sure to mark both front and back pattern pieces. Follow steps 2 to 5 on pages 78 and 79, sewing with the seam allowances designated by your pattern. It is not necessary to finish seams on knit skirts.

TIP: Read your pattern directions. Some patterns, especially those that have 1/4" (6 mm) seam allowances, instruct you to sew your elastic waistline with this method. There is no need to alter those patterns, as they already allow this amount of fabric at the top.

2. Cut a piece of elastic to fit your waist snugly, yet still stretch to fit over your hips. Overlap the ends 1/2" (1.3 cm), and stitch them together, using a wide zigzag stitch or multistitch-zigzag. Divide both the elastic and the upper edge of the skirt into fourths, and pin-mark. Pin the elastic to the wrong side of the skirt, aligning the edges and matching the pin marks; insert the pins perpendicular to the edges.

Quick Reference

Mark the hem length. During the marking, stand straight, wearing the shoes you will be wearing with the skirt. The person marking should measure up from the floor to the desired length, moving around you as necessary. Otherwise, the hem will be uneven. If you don't have help, turn up the hem to the desired length all the way around and check in a mirror for even length.

Twice the width of the elastic. For this method, 1" (2.5 cm) elastic works well, though you may decide to use a different width. Some specialty elastics have channels for topstitching, giving the look of multiple rows.

continued

Alternate Steps for a Knit Pull-on Skirt *continued*

Quick Reference

Stretching the elastic to fit between the pins. Grasp the fabric and elastic behind the presser foot with one hand and ahead of the presser foot with the other hand, working in small sections at a time. Stretch the elastic only far enough to take up the slack in the fabric. Keep an even tension on the elastic, allowing the feed dogs to feed the fabric at a steady pace. Stop sewing to move your hands.

3 Insert four more pins, evenly spaced, between the quarter marks, distributing the fabric fullness evenly. Set your machine for a medium-width multistitch-zigzag. Place the skirt under the presser foot with the elastic on top. Align the edge of the foot to the elastic and fabric edges. Stitch, **stretching the elastic to fit between the pins** and keeping the edges aligned. Remove pins as you come to them, stopping with the needle down in the fabric.

4 Fold the elastic to the wrong side of the skirt, so the fabric encases the elastic. From the right side of the skirt, **stitch in the ditch (p. 57)** of the seam through all the waistband layers, at each seam. This step makes step 5 easier.

TIP: Stretch the waistband slightly to give yourself a clear view of your target.

5 With the right side facing up, **TOP-STITCH** through all layers of the waistband, stretching the elastic as you sew. Use either a zigzag or multistitch-zigzag, with medium width and length, and stitch near the lower edge of the elastic. These stitches will allow the skirt to stretch as it goes over your hips. Finish the skirt, following steps 13 and 14 on page 82.

Simple Skirt
VARIATIONS

For woven skirts, sew multiple-channel casings to handle two rows of 3/8" (1 cm) elastic or three rows of 1/4" (6 mm) elastic. See the directions for pull-on-pants (page 87). To create this look with knit fabric, sew in one circle of wide elastic that has channels for topstitching (page 30).

Vary the hem treatment (page 22) to suit the skirt style or to add design interest. A narrow, double-fold hem is suitable for a slightly flared skirt. Use a double-needle hem to give knits a little stretch. Stitch invisible hems in dressy skirts, either by hand or by machine.

Pull-on Pants

Pull-on pants with elastic waists are easy to fit and easy to sew. When sewn in supple, light-weight wovens, such as rayon or microfiber, they are elegant enough for evening wear. For sportier looks, cotton, cotton blends, linen, or seersucker work well and can be paired with  simple T-shirts or blouses. Consider purchasing enough fabric to make a matching jacket or vest to go with your pants and complete the outfit.

Select a pants pattern with two main pieces: the front and the back. The elastic **CASING** for the waist is formed from excess fabric at the top. These instructions are for pants without pockets. The method for sewing side-seam pockets varies greatly from pattern to pattern. Once you understand the basics of sewing pull-on pants, you can advance to a pattern with pockets, following the pattern instructions closely.

WHAT YOU'LL LEARN	WHAT YOU'LL NEED
How to alter the crotch length of a pattern	Pants pattern; loose-fitting with elastic waistline
How to alter the leg length of a pattern	Fabric (check pattern for amount)
How to make a multi-row elastic waistband	Matching all-purpose thread
	3/8" (1 cm) elastic, enough to go twice around your waist

Let's Begin

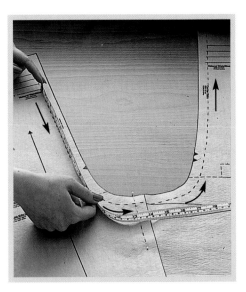

1 Measure the length of the crotch seam on a pair of pants that you know fits comfortably. Start from the bottom of the waistband in the front and measure the distance around the crotch to the bottom of the waistband in the back. On your pattern, measure the total crotch length, standing the tape measure on edge and measuring along the seamline of the center front and center back. Begin and end at the waistline mark; don't include the 5/8" (1.5 cm) **SEAM ALLOWANCES** at the inseam.

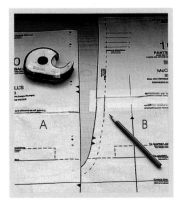

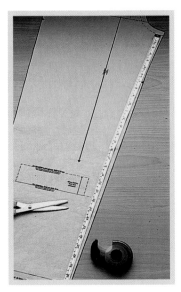

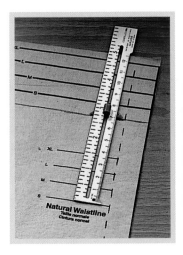

2 Compare the pants crotch length to the pattern crotch length. Alter your pattern, if necessary. Cut the pattern pieces apart on the horizontal adjustment line. Then lap the pieces **by half the total amount needed** to shorten **(A),** or separate the pieces by half the total amount needed to lengthen **(B).** Insert a paper strip to lengthen; tape the pieces in place.

3 Next, compare the inseam measurements on your pants and on your pattern, measuring from the crotch seamline to the hemline. Make any necessary alteration at the horizontal adjustment line.

4 To construct the pants following these directions, 2¾" (7 cm) of fabric must be allowed for the casing above the waistline. Measure this distance from the waistline, and mark a new cutting line on your pattern. (Add extra paper, if necessary.) Be sure to mark both front and back pattern pieces.

Quick Reference

By half the total amount needed. For example, if you need to lengthen the crotch 1" (2.5 cm), shorten the pants front 1/2" (1.3 cm), and shorten the pants back 1/2" (1.3 cm).

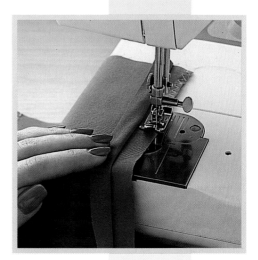

5 Prepare the fabric (page 37), lay out the pattern (page 44), and cut the fabric (page 48). Transfer any necessary marks (page 49). Set your sewing machine on a straight stitch of 10 to 12 stitches per inch, which is 2 to 2.5 mm. Insert a sewing machine needle suitable for your fabric (page 8). Place the right front over the right back, right sides together, along the inner leg. Pin them together, matching notches and inserting the pins perpendicular to the edges. Stitch the **SEAM,** using 5/8" (1.5 cm) seam allowance unless your pattern indicates another seam allowance. Repeat for the left front and back legs.

6 **FINISH** the edges of the seam allowances (page 19). **PRESS** the seams flat; then press them open.

7 With right sides together, pin the sewn right and left pants sections together at the crotch seam. Line up the inner leg seams, and match any notches. Stitch the entire seam. Then stitch the curved area of the seam between the notches a second time, 1/4" (6 mm) from the first stitching.

continued

continued

 Trim the seam in the curved area of the crotch close to the second stitching line. Finish the trimmed seam allowances. Then also finish the remaining seam allowances separately. Press the seam allowances open in the front and back, above the trimmed portion of the seam.

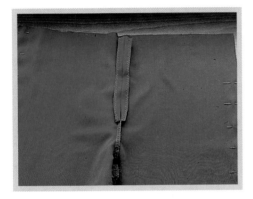

Pin the front and back, right sides together, at the side seams, matching notches and any other marks. Stitch a 5/8" (1.5 cm) seam from the bottom of the leg to the upper edge. Repeat for the other side seam.

Finish the seam allowances separately. Press the seams flat; then press them open, using a seam roll. **BASTE** all the seam allowances open flat from the upper edge down about 4" (10 cm). This will keep them from getting in the way when you insert the elastic in step 15.

Finish the waistline (page 19). Fold the upper edge 1 1/2" (3.8 cm) to the wrong side, and press. Insert pins along and perpendicular to the fold.

EDGESTITCH close to the fold around the upper edge of the waistline. Begin and end at a side seam, overlapping the stitches about 1/2" (1.3 cm).

Place a piece of tape on the bed of your machine 1 1/4" (3.2 cm) from the tip of the needle. Stitch the lower edge of the casing, guiding the upper edge along the tape. Leave a 2" (5 cm) opening at one side seam.

Measure from the upper edge of the waist to a point halfway between the two stitching lines. Place tape on the machine bed as a sewing guide. Stitch, leaving a 2" (5 cm) opening just above the first opening.

TIP: To use three rows of 1/4" (6 mm) elastic in your waistline casing, divide the space into even thirds.

Cut two pieces of 3/8" (1 cm) elastic a little larger than your waist measurement. Fasten a safety pin or bodkin (page 30) to one end of one elastic, and insert the elastic through the casing opening into the top channel. Push and pull the safety pin through all the way to the opposite side of the opening, taking care not to let the free end disappear into the opening. Then do the same with the second piece of elastic, inserting it into the lower channel. Secure the ends of both pieces with safety pins.

continued

continued

16 Try on the pants. Pull up the elastic to fit your waist snugly, yet comfortably; pin the ends together. Take off the pants. Pull the pinned ends of the top elastic several inches (centimeters) out of the casing. Trim the overlapped ends to 1/2" (1.3 cm), if necessary. Place them under the presser foot, and stitch through both layers, using a multistitch-zigzag. Repeat for the lower elastic.

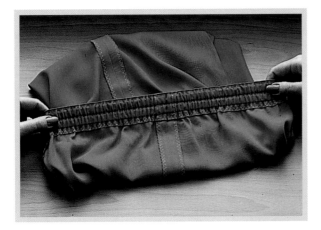

17 Machine-stitch the openings in the casing closed. Distribute the casing fullness evenly around the elastic. ***Stitch in the ditch (p. 57)*** at the seams to keep the elastic from shifting or rolling. Remove the basting stitches from step 10.

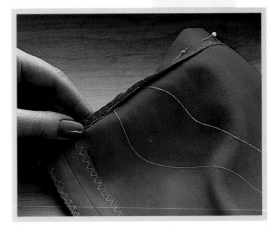

18 Turn under the hem allowance, and pin in place. Try on the pants, and adjust the length, if necessary. Take off the pants, and trim the hem allowance to an even depth. Press the fold. **FINISH** the lower edge. Stitch the hem by hand (page 22) or by machine (page 23). Give the pants a final pressing, and they're ready to wear!

MORE STYLES OF
Pull-on Pants

You'll find pants with various leg widths. These instructions work for pull-on shorts and culottes, too.

Vests

Vests, in a variety of styles, enhance wardrobes by complementing skirts, slacks, or dresses. They can be worn over knit tops, turtlenecks, or blouses, to fit the occasion.

For easy sewing, we've selected a loose-fitting, lined vest. Look for a pattern with two main pattern pieces: a front and a back. Good choices of fabric for a loose-fitting vest include cotton, cotton blends, rayon, linen, denim, wool crepe, wool gabardine, and corduroy. Select lining fabric made specifically for that purpose, or use lightweight cotton or blends.

WHAT YOU'LL LEARN

How to sew lining
in a vest

How to sew
buttonholes

How to sew on buttons

WHAT YOU'LL NEED

Vest pattern; lined, loose-fitting, with button closure

Fabric for vest (check pattern for amount)

Lining fabric (check pattern for amount)

Matching all-purpose thread

Lightweight to medium-weight fusible **INTER-FACING** (enough to back entire vest front)

Buttons

Let's Begin

1 Prepare the fabric (page 37). Lay out the pattern and cut the fabric (page 48) for the vest back pieces, reserving enough fabric for the fronts. Fuse interfacing to the wrong side of the vest front fabric, **following the manufacturer's directions (p. 55).** Lift and move the iron as needed to cover the entire piece. This will give support to buttons and buttonholes.

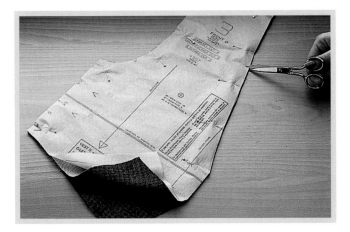

2 Lay out the vest front pieces on the interfaced fabric; cut. Lay out and cut the lining pieces. Transfer any necessary marks (page 49). Set your sewing machine on a straight stitch of 10 to 12 stitches per inch, which equals 2 to 2.5 mm. For most fabrics, a universal machine needle size 12/80 will work fine.

3 Place the vest fronts over the vest back, right sides together, aligning the shoulder **SEAM ALLOWANCE** edges and matching any notches. Insert pins along the shoulders, perpendicular to the cut edges. Stitch 5/8" (1.5 cm) shoulder **SEAMS**, *backstitching (p. 17)* at the beginning and end and removing the pins as you come to them.

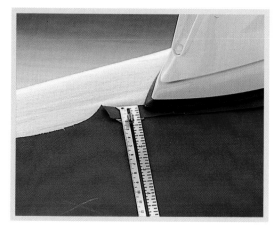

Quick Reference

Press the lining side seam allowances under 5/8" (1.5 cm). You'll understand the importance of this when you get to steps 14 and 15. It is much easier to measure and press under the side seam allowances of the lining now, but unfold them to complete the next few steps.

 Repeat step 3 for the lining pieces. For both the vest and the lining, **PRESS** the shoulder seams flat; then press them open. Also, *press the lining side seam allowances under 5/8" (1.5 cm).*

TIP: Because all the seam allowances are going to be enclosed between the vest and the lining, it is not necessary to **FINISH** them.

 Place the vest and the lining right sides together, matching the raw edges and any notches. Insert pins perpendicular to the edges along all but the side seams.

Stitch the 5/8" (1.5 cm) seam across the bottom of the vest back. Then stitch the armhole seams.

continued

continued

7 Beginning at the lower edge of one side, stitch one continuous seam along the bottom and center edges of one vest front, around the back neckline, and around the center and bottom edges of the other vest front, ending at the lower edge of the opposite side. Stop with the needle down in the fabric to pivot at each corner.

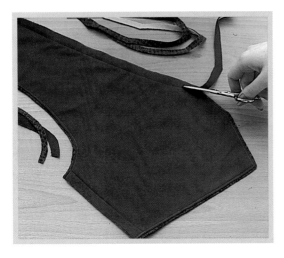

8 Trim the vest seam allowances to ¼" (6 mm); trim the lining seam allowances to ⅛" (3 mm). This step, called **GRADING**, reduces bulk. Do not trim the side seam allowances.

TIP: Trimming to these widths works well for tightly woven fabrics like this wool. For looser weaves that tend to ravel easily, trim the seam allowances wider.

9 **CLIP** into the curved neckline and armhole seam allowances every ½" (1.3 cm), clipping up to, but not through, the stitches. Clipping allows the seam allowance to turn smoothly to the inside and lie flat.

10 Put your hand through one of the open side seams of the back and through the shoulder of that side; grab the front of the vest. Pull it through the lining and vest at the shoulder and out the side seam, turning it right side out. Turn the other front right side out through the same side opening. Turn the back right side out.

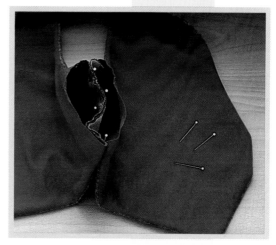

11 Insert a point turner (page 31) or similar tool into an opening, and gently push out any corners as necessary. Press all the seamed edges of the vest, centering the seam on the edge, with the lining to the inside.

12 Pin the vest front and back, right sides together, along the side seams, keeping the lining free. Match up the armhole seams, placing a pin directly in the seamline and turning the seam allowances toward the lining. Match up the lower seams in the same way. Then pin the lining front and back together 1" to 2" (2.5 to 5 cm) beyond the seams.

continued

continued

13 Sew a ⅝" (1.5 cm) seam where you have pinned, **backstitching (p. 17)** at each end. As you cross the seam allowances at the armhole and lower edge, keep them turned toward the lining; remove pins as you come to them.

TIP: This is an awkward seam to sew, especially at the beginning and end. Use the pressed foldlines of the lining (step 4) as seam guides there. Take your time, and be careful to keep the rest of the vest out of the way so that you do not catch unwanted-ed fabric in the stitches.

14 With your fingers, press the seam allowances open; turn in the lining seam allowances along the previously pressed lines. Press with your iron.

15 Pin the openings in the lining side seams closed. Slipstitch the edges together as on page 20.

16 **TOPSTITCH** ⅜" (1 cm) from the edge, around the armholes and around the lower, front, and neck edges.

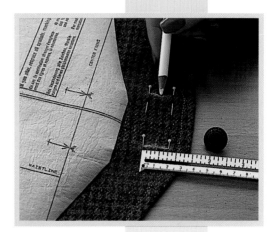

17 Transfer the buttonhole markings from your pattern to the vest (page 49). Make sure they are all the same distance from the front edge and uniform in size. Usually a buttonhole is 1/8" (3 mm) longer than the button diameter. To sew the buttonholes, follow the instructions in your sewing machine manual.

TIP: Remember, buttonholes go on the right front for females or on the left front for males. Don't cut them open until you have double-checked for accuracy in placement and size.

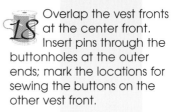18 Overlap the vest fronts at the center front. Insert pins through the buttonholes at the outer ends; mark the locations for sewing the buttons on the other vest front.

19 Sew on the buttons as on page 21.

TIP: Running thread through beeswax before sewing on the buttons will make the thread stronger and help prevent it from tangling. After running the thread through beeswax, run it through your fingers to melt the wax into the thread.

Vest
VARIATIONS

Make a
reversible vest
by lining it with a
fabric that can be
worn on the outside
rather than with lining fabric.
Omit buttons and buttonholes,
or sew sets of buttons to each side.

Vests have become the palette for
a variety of artistic techniques. Add
embroidery, beading, or painting
to personalize your vest.
Lining fabric is often
used for both the
inside and the out-
side of the
vest back.

Before lining your vest, sew **PATCH POCKETS** *to the fronts, following steps 2 to 6 on pages 114 and 115; see page 123 for rounded-corner pockets.*

Wrap Skirts

This wrap skirt is made from a rectangle of fabric; no pattern is needed. The rectangle size is determined from your own measurements, so the skirt is sure to fit. The upper edge is softly gathered onto a flat waistband, which is secured with a button closure.

A wrap skirt is the perfect candidate for a **BORDER-PRINT** fabric. The continuous design that runs along one **SELVAGE** becomes the lower edge of the skirt. Other suitable fabrics include solid colors and small, **NONDIRECTIONAL PRINTS.**

WHAT YOU'LL LEARN

How to **GATHER** fabric

How to sew a waistband

How to sew
double-fold hems

WHAT YOU'LL NEED

Border-print (optional) lightweight woven fabric, length determined in step 1

Perforated waistband interfacing, for 1¼" (3.2 cm) waistband, enough to go around your waist plus 12" (30.5 cm)

Matching all-purpose thread

Two buttons

Let's Begin

1 Measure your hips at the widest location. Add 18" (46 cm) to this measurement to determine the width (side to side) of the rectangle. This is also the amount of fabric you need to buy. Decide how long you want the skirt, from your waist to the hem, and add 1⅝" (4 cm), to determine the length (top to bottom) of the rectangle. Cut a rectangle of fabric with these measurements. If you are using a border print, cut the rectangle with the width running on the **LENGTHWISE GRAIN,** and the lower edge just above the **SELVAGE** on the border side.

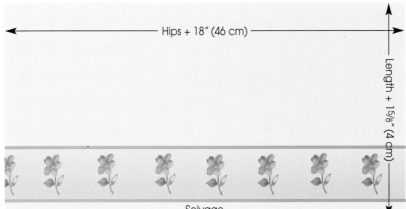

Hips + 18" (46 cm)

Length + 1⅝" (4 cm)

Selvage

2 Turn under the lower edge of the rectangle 1" (2.5 cm), and **PRESS.** Unfold the edge and turn the raw edge in to meet the pressed fold; press again. Then refold the edge, forming a ***double-fold hem.*** Insert pins perpendicular to the folds.

3 Stitch along the inner fold, removing the pins as you come to them. **EDGESTITCH** the outer fold.

Double-fold hem. Double-fold hems are made with two folds of equal depths, encasing the cut edge in the crease of the outer fold. Pressing the first fold to the total hem depth, in this case 1" (2.5 cm), allows you to be more accurate in turning and pressing.

4 Repeat steps 3 and 4 to hem each end of the rectangle, **backstitching (p. 17)** a few stitches at the bottom of the hems.

TIP: At this point, check to be sure that both short ends of the skirt rectangle are exactly the same length. If one is slightly longer, trim them off evenly at the top edge.

5 Set your machine to sew long straight stitches. Beginning at one side hem, stitch a scant 5/8" (1.5 cm) from the edge along the top of the rectangle, stitching from the right side of the fabric. Stop stitching at the opposite side hem. Stitch a second row of long stitches 1/4" (6 mm) closer to the edge. Leave thread tails at both ends.

TIP: To stitch the second row, guide the fabric with the first stitching row along the left edge of the presser foot.

continued

continued

6 Cut **perforated waistband interfacing** 12" (30.5 cm) longer than your waist measurement. Fuse the interfacing to the fabric, with the **wider side of the interfacing along the selvage.** Cut out the waistband, allowing 1/2" (1.3 cm) excess fabric at the ends and 5/8" (1.5 cm) on the long edge for **SEAM ALLOWANCES.**

7 Mark the cut edge of the waistband 1/2" (1.3 cm) from each end. Then divide the remaining length into four equal parts, and mark, using chalk pencil or erasable marker. Divide the upper edge of the skirt into four equal parts, and mark.

8 With right sides together, pin the cut edge of the waistband to the upper edge of the skirt, matching quarter marks. Insert pins from the skirt side. At one end, grasp both bobbin threads, and pull on them with equal tension, sliding the fabric along the thread to **GATHER** it.

Perforated waistband interfacing. You can buy this convenient product at the fabric store, by the yard (meter) or in prepackaged lengths. Check the product label to be sure it works with the waistband measurements given in these instructions. Or, use the measurements specified by the manufacturer.

Wider side of the interfacing along the selvage. Normally, you avoid using the selvage edge because it is more tightly woven than the rest of the fabric, and it may tend to pucker if used in a seam. However, for waistbands, using the selvage eliminates the need to **FINISH** the edge or turn it under, thus eliminating extra steps and extra bulk.

9 Keep pulling on the bobbin threads, gathering the fabric, and distributing the gathers evenly between the pins on half of the waistband. When the skirt fabric is gathered up to fit that half, secure the bobbin threads by winding them in a figure eight around the end pin.

10 Pull the bobbin threads from the other end to gather the remaining half; secure the threads. Distribute all the gathered fabric evenly along the waistband, inserting pins frequently to hold the fabric in place.

11 Reset the stitch length for 10 to 12 stitches per inch, which is 2 to 2.5 mm. Place the fabric under the presser foot, with the waistband on the bottom. Stitch 5/8" (1.5 cm) from the raw edges, keeping the gathers even and removing the pins as you come to them.

continued

continued

12 **GRADE** the seam allowances, by trimming the skirt seam allowance to ³/8" (1 cm), just above the gathering stitches.

13 Turn the seam allowance toward the waistband, and press lightly with tip of the iron. Avoid pressing creases into the gathers.

14 Fold the waistband on the interfacing center foldline, right sides together. The selvage edge extends down flat; the other edge is pressed up. Stitch ¹/2" (1.3 cm) from the edge at each end. Trim the seam allowances to ¹/4" (6 mm). Then trim the upper corners diagonally.

15 Turn the waistband right side out, and press. The selvage edge extends down over the seam on the wrong side. From the right side, pin in the ditch of the waistband seam, catching the selvage edge on the back. At the ends, turn the corner of the selvage under at an angle.

> **TIP:** Be sure to keep the seam allowance turned up as it was pressed. Check to be sure the selvage edge is pinned at a consistent depth and lies flat.

16 *Stitch in the ditch (p. 57)* of the seam from the right side of the skirt, backstitching at the ends and removing the pins as you come to them.

17 Try on the skirt, lapping the right side over the left side. Mark the waistband at each end, using a pin.

18 Stitch a buttonhole at each end of the waistband, following the directions in your owner's manual. Sew a button to the outside of the waistband on the left side; sew a button to the underside of the waistband on the right side.

Unlined *Jackets*

Collarless jackets are versatile additions to any wardrobe. Those that are loose-fitting and unlined, with **DROP-SHOULDER** styling and **PATCH POCKETS,** are easy to make. Look for a pattern that includes pieces for front, back, sleeve, front **FACING,** back facing, and pocket. These directions are for square bottom front corners. If your pattern has round corners, pay close attention to the pattern directions when attaching the facing (step 11) and hemming the lower edge (steps 24 to 27).

As with any other project, the fabric of your jacket will determine whether it will be more suitable for casual, business, or dress. Cotton, cotton blends, and denim would be good choices to wear with jeans or casual slacks and skirts. Wool, wool blends, linen, and rayon work for business or dress. When you're feeling really confident, you might even consider making a jacket of suit-weight silk, like the one at left.

WHAT YOU'LL LEARN

How to sew a drop-shoulder sleeve

How to sew a patch pocket

How to apply fusible **INTERFACING**

How to sew neck and front facings

WHAT YOU'LL NEED

Jacket pattern; unlined, loose-fitting

Fabric for jacket (check pattern for amount)

Matching all-purpose thread

Lightweight fusible interfacing (check pattern for amount)

Buttons

Let's Begin

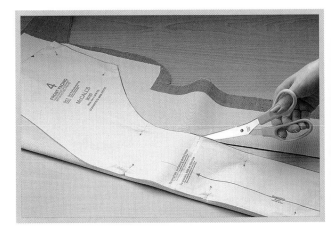

1 Prepare the fabric (page 37). Lay out the pattern pieces (page 44), and cut out (page 48) all but the facings. Fuse interfacing to the wrong side of the fabric for the facings, *following the manufacturer's directions (p. 55).* Then cut out the facings. Transfer any necessary marks (page 49).

2 Turn under the top edge of the pocket 1/4" (6 mm); **PRESS.** To **FINISH** the edge, set your machine for a zigzag stitch of medium length and width. Stitch close to the folded edge, so that the right-hand swing of the needle just clears the fold.

3 Turn the upper edge of the pocket (the facing) to the outside on the foldline; pin at the sides. Starting at the top of the pocket, stitch a 5/8" (1.5 cm) **SEAM** to the bottom of the facing on each side of the pocket, *backstitching (p. 17)* at the beginning and end. Trim the facing **SEAM ALLOWANCE** to 3/8" (1 cm). Trim the upper corners diagonally.

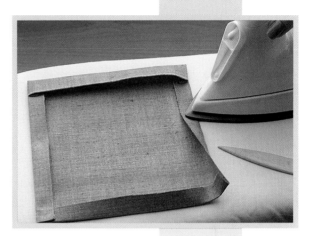

4 Turn the facing to the inside. Using a point turner or similar tool, gently push out the corners to square them off. Press the top fold. If the pocket has square bottom corners, turn under 5/8" (1.5 cm) on the bottom, and press. Then repeat for the side edges. For pockets with rounded corners, see the variation on page 123.

5 Set your sewing machine for a straight stitch of 10 to 12 stitches per inch, which is 2 to 2.5 mm. Measure the finished width of the facing; subtract 1/8" (3 mm). Mark this distance from the needle on the machine bed, using tape. **TOPSTITCH** the upper edge of the pocket, guiding the fold along the tape mark and catching the facing in the stitches.

6 Repeat steps 2 to 5 for the other pocket. Place the pockets on the jacket front, matching the upper corners to the markings transferred from the pattern. Pin them securely in place, inserting the pins perpendicular to the edges. **EDGESTITCH** around the sides and bottom of the pockets, backstitching at both upper corners. Stop with the needle down in the fabric to pivot at each corner. Remove the pins as you come to them.

continued

continued

7 Pin the jacket fronts to the jacket back at the shoulders, with right sides together, aligning the cut edges and matching any notches. Insert the pins perpendicular to the edges.

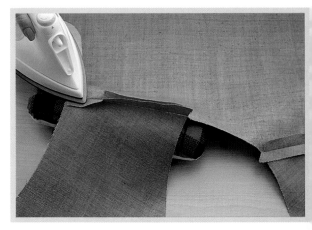

8 Stitch the seams, guiding the cut edges along the 5/8" (1.5 cm) seam allowance guide. Press the seams flat; then press them open.

9 Sew the front facings to the back facing at the shoulders as in steps 7 and 8. Trim the seam allowances to 1/4" (6 mm). Finish the inner, unnotched edges of the front facings and the lower edge of the back facing (arrows) as in step 2.

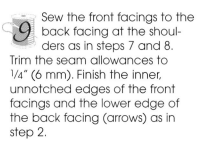

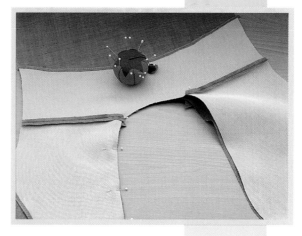

10 Pin the facing to the jacket, right sides together, aligning the cut edges. Match the shoulder seams and all notches. At the shoulders, insert a pin in the wells of the seams, to keep them aligned.

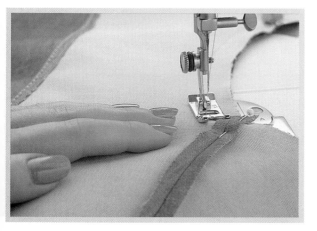

11 Stitch the facing to the jacket, guiding the cut edges along the 5/8" (1.5 cm) seam allowance guide. Stitch continuously from one lower edge, around the neckline, to the opposite lower edge; backstitch a few stitches at the beginning and end. Remove the pins as you come to them, and keep the shoulder seam allowances open flat.

12 GRADE the seam allowances by trimming the jacket neckline seam allowance to 3/8" (1 cm) and the facing seam allowance to 1/4" (6 mm). CLIP into the neckline seam allowance every 1/2" (1.3 cm), clipping up to, but not through, the stitches. Clipping allows the facing to turn smoothly to the inside and lie flat.

continued

continued

13 Press the seam allowances flat; then press them toward the facing. With the right side up, place the facing **(A)** under the presser foot, so the needle is aligned to enter the fabric just to the right of the seam at the lower left front; the jacket **(B)** extends off the left of the machine bed. Keeping the seam allowance turned toward the facing (arrows), stitch all around the fronts and neckline very close to the seam. You will be stitching through the facing and the seam allowance, but not through the jacket. This step, called **UNDER-STITCHING,** helps the facing lie flat.

TIP: Along the curve of the neckline, keep the facing lying flat, allowing the jacket to "bunch up" to the left of the curve. Stitch, following the curve of the facing. The clipped seam allowance will "fan out" underneath the facing.

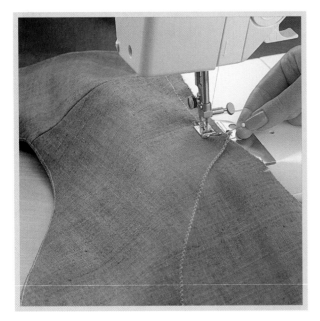

14 Turn the facing to the inside; press. Align the shoulder seams, and smooth them out to the sleeve edge. Pin the facing to the sleeve edge, inserting the pins perpendicular to the edge. Set your machine for long straight stitches. **BASTE** the facings to the sleeve edges.

TIP: Some jacket patterns have facings that do not extend all the way to the sleeve edge. Align the shoulder seam allowances, and *stitch in the ditch (p. 57)* to secure the facing to the jacket.

15 Pin the sleeve to the jacket, with right sides together. Align the cut edges, and match the notches. You probably also have a mark on the sleeve edge that aligns to the jacket shoulder seam. Count the notches to be sure you are pinning the correct sleeve. Pin frequently from the jacket side, easing the sleeve to fit smoothly.

16 Place the jacket under the presser foot, with the sleeve underneath. Stitch the seam, guiding the edges along the 5/8" (1.5 cm) seam allowance guide. Remove the pins as you come to them.

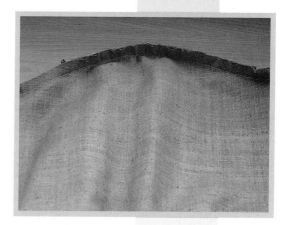

17 Check from the sleeve side, to be sure there are no puckers. If there are any, clip the stitches, using a seam ripper, and remove the stitches on either side of the pucker far enough to smooth it out; restitch.

18 Stitch a second line in the seam allowances, 1/4" (6 mm) from the first stitching line, from the notches to each end. Trim the seam allowances in this area close to the second stitching line.

continued

continued

19 Repeat steps 15 to 18 for the opposite sleeve. Set your machine for a medium-length, medium-width zigzag stitch. For each sleeve, finish the seam allowance edges together, stitching so that the right swing of the needle just clears the fabric edge. Press the seam allowances toward the sleeves.

20 Pin the jacket front to the jacket back, right sides together, along the side seams and extending on to the underarm sleeve seams. Match notches, and align the sleeve seams. Insert the pins perpendicular to the edges.

21 Stitch 5/8" (1.5 cm) seam from the bottom of one side continuously to the end of the sleeve. Keep the underarm seam allowances turned toward the sleeve. Repeat for the opposite side.

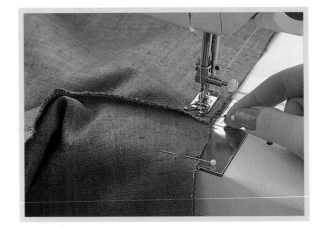

Finish the side and underarm seam allowances as in step 2. Press the seam allowances flat; then press them open.

TIP: Press the seam allowances open over a seam roll to prevent imprinting the seam allowance edges onto the right side of the jacket and to make it easier to press the sleeve seams open.

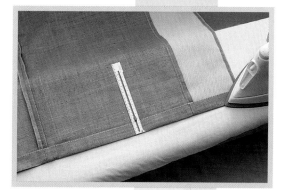

 Finish the lower edge of the jacket as in step 2. Repeat for the lower edges of the sleeves. Turn under the remaining hem allowances on the sleeves, and press, using a seam roll or sleeve board (page 29). Slipstitch (page 20) the hems to the jacket.

Place the jacket on your ironing board, wrong side up; open the front facings. Turn under the remaining hem allowance on the lower edge, including the facings; press.

Unfold the lower edge. Turn the jacket over, and turn the facing to the outside, aligning the lower edges. Pin, keeping the facing seam allowances turned toward the facing. Stitch the facing to the jacket, stitching in the well of the pressed fold. Repeat for the opposite side.

continued

continued

 Trim the facing seam allowance to within 1/4" (6 mm) of the stitches. Trim the corner diagonally, to within 1/8" (3 mm) of the corner stitch. Repeat for the opposite side. Turn the facings to the inside, and press.

 Refold the remaining hem, and pin. Slipstitch the hem to the jacket. At the fronts, slipstitch the facings to the hem.

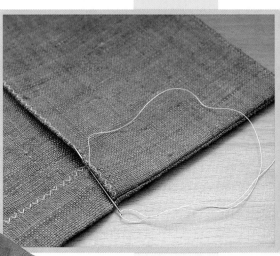

TOPSTITCH 3/8" (1 cm) from the edges along the fronts and neckline of the jacket, if desired. If your jacket has buttons, transfer the buttonhole placement marks from your pattern to the right jacket front. Make buttonholes, following the directions in your sewing machine owner's manual. Transfer the button placement marks to the left front. Sew buttons as on page 21.

Jacket Variations

Some jackets do not overlap at the front, but merely meet at the center. For these styles, you can add decorative closures, such as purchased frogs, toggles, or clips.

For pockets with round corners, machine-baste 1/4" (6 mm) from the raw edge around the bottom corners. Make a cardboard template to help you get the sides of the pocket folded in and pressed evenly. Cut the template the size and shape of the finished pocket (the size of the pattern piece minus the seam allowances and facing). Before top-stitching the facing, lay the template over the inside of the pocket, and push it up to the top under the facing. Press all the raw edges over the template, pulling up the basting threads around the corners to draw in the curves.

Glossary

BASTE. Long, easy-to-remove stitches are sewn into the fabric temporarily, either by hand or by machine. Hand-basting stitches are used to hold layers of fabric together before permanent stitching. Machine-basting stitches are used to gather a section of fabric into a smaller space.

BIAS. Any diagonal line intersecting the lengthwise and crosswise grains of fabric is referred to as *bias*. While woven fabric does not stretch on the lengthwise and crosswise grains, it has considerable stretch in the direction of the bias.

BORDER PRINT. Fabric is printed with a bold pattern, usually larger in scale than the rest of the design, running along one selvage. The border pattern is often used along the hemline in a garment, which means the lengthwise grain of the fabric runs horizontally on the garment.

CASING. A fabric tunnel is sewn into the garment, often at the waistline, to carry elastic or cording.

CLIPPING. Small, closely spaced cuts are made into the seam allowances of a garment, usually along a curve or into a corner. When the garment is turned right side out, the seam allowances can spread apart and lie flat where they have been clipped. Small clips are also used for marking notches or dots from the pattern to the fabric.

COURSES. Corresponding to the crosswise grain of a woven fabric, the courses of a knit fabric run perpendicular to the selvages and ribs. Knit fabrics are most stretchy in the direction of the courses.

CROSSWISE GRAIN. On woven fabric, the crosswise grain runs perpendicular to the selvages. Fabric has slight "give" in the crosswise grain.

DROP-SHOULDER. This garment design feature means that the seam joining the sleeve to the front and back is intended to fall down off the edge of the shoulder, rather than align to the shoulder crest. Drop-shoulder styles are rather relaxed, less fitted, and generally have more room in the armhole.

EDGESTITCH. With the machine set for straight stitching at a length of 2 to 2.5 mm or 10 to 12 stitches per inch, stitch within 1/8" (3 mm) of the finished edge of a neckline, hem, or similar feature. With many machines, this can be achieved by guiding the inner edge of the right presser foot toe along the outer edge of the garment.

FACING. A fabric extension or addition that is sewn as a backing to another piece protects raw edges of seam allowances from raveling and gives the item a neat, finished appearance. For instance, a jacket front and neckline have an outer layer and an under-layer, or *facing*.

FINISH. To improve the durability of a seam, facing, or hem, the raw edge is secured in one of several stitching methods that prevents it from raveling. Zigzag, multistitch-zigzag, and pinking are some of the ways to finish seam allowances.

FREE ARM. Many sewing machines are designed with a narrow, freestanding bed that allows for easy access to tight areas, such as sewing ribbing to a neckline or sleeve, hemming pant legs, or sewing inside a cylinder.

GATHER. Two rows of long stitches are sewn along a seamline. When the bobbin threads are pulled, the fabric slides along the stitches into tiny tucks. Gathers are used to fit a wide garment section to a narrower section while at the same time adding shaping.

GRADING. Seam allowances on faced edges are trimmed to graduated widths to eliminate a bulky ridge. Often the garment seam allowance is trimmed to 1/4" (6 mm) and the facing seam allowance is trimmed to 1/8" (3 mm).

INTERFACING. This product is available in many weights, and in woven, knit, and non-woven forms. It stiffens fabric, gives it support, and prevents it from stretching out of shape. Some forms are heat-fused to the wrong side of the fabric.

LENGTHWISE GRAIN. On woven fabric, the lengthwise grain runs parallel to the selvages. It is the strongest direction of the fabric with the least amount of "give."

NAP. Some fabrics have definite "up" and "down" directions, either because of a surface pile, like corduroy or velveteen, or because of a one-way print. When laying out the pattern on napped fabric, cut all the pieces with the top edges facing the same direction.

NONDIRECTIONAL PRINT. The design printed on the fabric has no definite "up" and "down" directions, and pattern pieces can be laid out with the top edges facing in either direction.

PATCH POCKETS. One of the easiest pocket styles to sew, these are sewn to the outer surface of the garment like a "patch."

PRESSING. This step is extremely important to the success of your sewing projects. Select the heat setting appropriate for your fabric, and use steam. Lift and lower the iron in an overlapping pattern. Do not slide the iron down the seam, as this can cause the fabric to stretch out of shape, especially on the crosswise grain or bias.

RIBS. Corresponding to the lengthwise grain in woven fabric, the ribs of a knit fabric run parallel to the selvages (if there are any). Knits are usually most stable in the rib direction.

RIBBING. A very stretchy knit fabric, usually with pronounced ribs. It is especially suitable for necks and cuffs on knit garments, since it can easily stretch to go over heads and hands, yet spring back in shape once in place. Most ribbing comes in much narrower

widths than other fabrics and, because you use less of it, it is generally sold by the inch (centimeter) rather than the yard (meter).

SEAM. Two pieces of fabric are placed right sides together and joined along the edge with stitches. After stitching, the raw edges are hidden on the wrong side, leaving a clean, smooth line on the right side.

SEAM ALLOWANCE. Narrow excess fabric lies between the stitching line and the raw edge. Stitching with a 5/8" (1.5 cm) seam allowance on woven fabrics gives the seam strength and ensures that the stitches cannot be pulled off the raw edges. Knits, which do not ravel, are usually sewn with 1/4" (6 mm) seam allowances.

SELVAGES. Characteristic of woven fabrics, this narrow, tightly woven outer edge should usually be cut away. Avoid the temptation to use it as a seam edge because it may cause the seam to pucker and may shrink excessively when washed. However, the selvage is useful as a finished edge on a flat waistband.

STAYSTITCHING is a line of regular straight stitching placed 1/2" (1.3 cm) from the seam edge on a single layer of fabric. Used on curves or when the seamline is cut on the bias, its purpose is to prevent the fabric edge from stretching out of shape before it is sewn into a seam.

TOPSTITCH. A decorative and functional stitching line placed 1/4" to 1" (6 mm to 2.5 cm) from the finished edge of a neckline, jacket front, pocket facing, or similar garment feature. The stitching is done with the right side of the garment facing up. Sometimes topstitching is done with heavier thread or two threads through the machine needle, to make it more visible.

UNDERSTITCHING is straight stitching very close to the seamline that connects a facing to the garment. After the seam allowances are trimmed, clipped, and pressed toward the facing, stitch from the right side of the facing to keep it from rolling to the right side.

Index

CREATIVE
PUBLISHING
international

President: Iain Macfarlane
Group Director, Book Development: Zoe Graul
Director, Creative Development: Lisa Rosenthal
Executive Managing Editor: Elaine Perry

Project Manager: Amy Friebe
Senior Editor: Linda Neubauer
Senior Art Director: Delores Swanson
Assisting Art Director: Mark Jacobson
Writers: Linda Hanner, Linda Neubauer
Copy Editor: Janice Cauley
Researcher: Louise Mensing
Lead Project & Prop Stylist: Joanne Wawra
Project & Prop Stylist: Coralie Sathre
Sample Production Manager:
  Elizabeth Reichow
Lead Samplemaker: Phyllis Galbraith
Sewing Staff: Arlene Dohrman, Sheila Duffy,
  Sharon Eklund, Teresa Henn, Muriel Lynch,
  Dolores Minkema, Nancy Sundeen,
  Joan Wigginton
Senior Technical Photo Stylist: Bridget Haugh
Technical Photo Stylists: Sharon Eklund,
  Nancy Sundeen
Studio Services Manager: Marcia Chambers
Photo Services Coordinator: Carol Osterhus
Photographer: Chuck Nields
Photography Assistant: Andrea Rugg
Manager, Production Services: Kim Gerber
Mac Design Manager: Jon Simpson
Mac Designers: Eileen Bovard, Laurie Kristensen,
  Brad Webster
Production Staff: Curt Ellering, Laura Hokkanen,
  Kay Wethern
Consultant: Teresa Henn
Contributors: Coats & Clark Inc.; Handler
  Textile Corporation; Kwik-Sew® Pattern Co.,
  Inc.; The McCall Pattern Company;
  Olfa® Products Group/Division of General
  Housewares Corporation

Printed on American paper by:
  R. R. Donnelley & Sons Co.
01 00 99 98 / 5 4 3 2 1

Creative Publishing international, Inc.
  offers a variety of how-to books. For
  information write:
        Creative Publishing international, Inc.
        Subscriber Books
        5900 Green Oak Drive
        Minnetonka, MN 55343